What people are saying about …

D0430081

Speaking of Jesus

"*Speaking of Jesus* is a beautifully framed rethink on what it means to champion Jesus. In the most readable and practical fashion, Carl gives thoughtful answers for engaging the world, but more importantly, you'll find a compass by which you can faithfully follow Jesus and help others find Him … anywhere in the world."

Hugh Halter, author of
The Tangible Kingdom and *Sacrilege*

"You may not agree with everything in this book. I don't. But you will be moved by it as I was. Carl's Jesus is an irresistibly compelling figure, and Carl's way of speaking of Jesus is immensely attractive."

Miroslav Volf, Henry B. Wright Professor of
Systematic Theology at Yale Divinity School,
founding director of Yale Center for Faith and
Culture, and author of *Allah: A Christian Response*

"Is your life driven more by Christian culture or following Jesus? How sure are you of your answer? In *Speaking of Jesus*, Carl Medearis takes a thought-provoking and compelling look at the difference and the tragic consequences to the Jesus movement locally and globally if we get it wrong. Read every word if you care most about fully living the adventure Jesus intended when He first asked you to follow Him."

Jim Mellado, president of
Willow Creek Association

"Provocative, engaging, and practical, *Speaking of Jesus* is a clear and compelling call to rethink the traditional approach to pointing people to Christ. Carl Medearis outlines a refreshing evangelism paradigm shift relevant for today's culture."

Garry Poole, evangelism consultant
and author of *Seeker Small Groups*

"*Speaking of Jesus* is a poignant and provocative message for all Christians of all persuasions. What the world needs now is not more Christians, but people who think and talk and act like Jesus. Carl's message is a prophetic reminder that Jesus did not come into the world to found the Christian religion but to embrace people from every tribe and type in the Father's love. *Speaking of Jesus* is the most relevant and powerful expression of the gospel I have read."

Ron Nikkel, president of Prison
Fellowship International

"You don't have to be dishonest about who you are to share who Jesus is. The gospel message must be born in truth just as Jesus was. If people would take what Carl writes seriously, it would radically change how we talk about Jesus and how others see Him. You don't have to agree with Carl—but if you fail to wrestle with the questions he raises, you will not be effective in your speaking of Jesus."

Bob Roberts Jr., senior pastor of NorthWood
Church, global strategist, speaker, and
author of *Real-Time Connections*

"With every page of this book I breathed a sigh of relief. Carl reminds me that it's when I am speaking of Jesus that I am sharing the good news of my salvation, and this is not a rescue that religion has to offer."

Sarah Macintosh, singer/songwriter,
formerly of Chasing Furies

"One of the great questions of our time is whether faith is going to be a bridge of cooperation or a barrier of division. In this illuminating book, Carl Medearis offers us a powerful way to build bridges. It's simple, really: Follow the carpenter. Follow Jesus. Follow his way of radical love and inclusive community. Thank you, Carl, for bringing us together in such a beautiful, simple way."

Dr. Eboo Patel, founder and president of
Interfaith Youth Core and author of *Acts of Faith*

"This book will not make you comfortable. It will challenge you, test your core beliefs, and cause you to reconsider how you have presented the good news of Jesus."

Brady Boyd, pastor of New Life
Church and author of *Fear No Evil*

speaking of
Jesus

To Ken & Kathy

speaking of
Jesus

the art of **not**-evangelism

carl medearis

David C Cook®
transforming lives together

SPEAKING OF JESUS
Published by David C Cook
4050 Lee Vance View
Colorado Springs, CO 80918 U.S.A.

David C Cook Distribution Canada
55 Woodslee Avenue, Paris, Ontario, Canada N3L 3E5

David C Cook U.K., Kingsway Communications
Eastbourne, East Sussex BN23 6NT, England

The graphic circle C logo is a registered trademark of David C Cook.

The website addresses recommended throughout this book are offered as a
resource to you. These websites are not intended in any way to be or imply an
endorsement on the part of David C Cook, nor do we vouch for their content.

LCCN 2011920250
ISBN 978-1-4347-0210-4
eISBN 978-0-7814-0626-0

© 2011 Carl Medearis
Published in association with the literary agency of Creative Trust, Inc.,
5141 Virginia Way, Suite 320, Brentwood, TN 37027.

The Team: Don Pape, John Blase, Sarah Schultz, Renada Arens, and Karen Athen
Cover Design: Amy Kiechlin Konyndyk
Cover Photo: iStockphoto 9299481

Printed in the United States of America
First Edition 2011

4 5 6 7 8 9 10

032713

*To Chris. You speak of Jesus as purely
and simply as anyone I know.*

The story is told of the Sunday-school teacher who was having a tough time getting her class to participate. So she decided to ask an easy question: "What's gray, has a bushy tail, and stores nuts for the winter?" The children looked at one another and didn't say a word. Finally, brave little Johnny raised his hand and said, "I know the answer must be Jesus, but it sure sounds like a squirrel to me."

It seems to me that we all are like little Johnny—we all know the answer is Jesus. We believe it. We say it. Yet, woefully, perhaps shamefully, our answers tend to be scripted even when they don't make sense. I hope that in the following pages I can help you overcome that.

Contents

Introduction   15

1. What's Missing in This Gospel?   21

2. Unfair Advantage   33

3. Owning Christianity   45

4. In or Out   63

5. What Would Paul Say?   77

6. Speak of Jesus ... Not about Jesus   87

7. Our Religion Can Beat Up Your Religion!   97

8. Is It Good News?   107

9. You're Under Arrest ... for Speaking Christianese!   119

10. Jesus the Folk Hero   131

11. Confused about Jesus ... and That's Okay!   143

12. Gays, Liberals, and Muslims   157

Appendix   179

Notes   185

Introduction

Imagine yourself on a soccer team. You're the goalie. You're a major part of Team Christian.

Your opponent is known as the Rest-of-the-World All-Star Team, pulled together from the top teams around the planet. Its captain is the leading scorer on the formidable Team Muslim. The others are mostly from Team Hindu and Team Secular Humanist, with a single member—the striker—from Team Atheist. Team Christian scores first with an amazing header by one of the stars from the Evangelical Squad, originally out of the Dallas, Texas, area. But in the twelfth minute, one of the Muslims from the Rest-of-the-World All-Star Team scores. The game goes into half-time tied at 1–1.

You see the coach is obviously nervous. "This is it," he yells. "It's the final half. Of course, we know that in the end the greatest soccer player of all time will come back and win it for us, but in the mean-time we can't let up. We can't let him down!"

Some of the players chime in that really all that's needed is to be faithful. "We just can't give up," some say. "If we don't give up, it'll all work out in the end."

Others insist that this isn't the whole story. "We have been given the responsibility to win this game. We need a clear strategy. Faithfulness is good, but it doesn't guarantee a win. And we *must* win."

One of the young, new players stands up and in a moment of passion blurts out, "Let's kill 'em. I mean, not literally, but we need to take it to 'em. No holding back. Just run 'em over. Whatever it takes. *Win.*"

Then you, one of the oldest members of the team, originally from one of the old-school denominational squads, stand and calmly state, "Listen. This isn't easy, I know. But we don't just need better strategy. More faithfulness. Or simply trying harder. We need to befriend them. Be nice to them. Maybe share some hugs or handshakes. Be caring. Then they'll trust us and we can score more easily."

The players murmur with assent. That is wisdom. We can't just beat them over the head with the soccer ball. We have to be nice, *then* they will see. And if our teams can just get along long enough … we'll *win* them.

The second half starts. Team Christian employs a mix of all three things: not giving up, trying harder, and being nicer. Whatever it is, Team Christian scores the next goal only two minutes into the second half.

Then something unthinkable happens. You see a man walking straight across the field. He's not part of the game. He's in sandals. The ref blows his whistle and starts to run at the man to get him off the pitch. Just before he reaches the other side, the man stops and looks right at you. *You.* The one keeping goal. He sees you. Even though he's a good fifty yards away, somehow you can see his eyes. They seem like they are on fire. Passion. Or power. Or … is it compassion? But there's something about his eyes. Strange. You've never seen him before. He doesn't look like he's from around these parts. Then …

He calls your name. Not loudly, but clearly. "Come. Follow me."

What? you think to yourself. *Who does he think he is? Is he blind? Can he not see that I'm keeping the goal in the most important game of all time? We're up 2–1 with about fifteen minutes left.*

But he simply turns and walks on. Obviously going somewhere. Where? Who is this guy and what does he think he's doing interrupting this game of a lifetime?

But his eyes pierced right through you. You never felt that before. You can't describe it, but you have to at least know who he is and where he's going. To the shock of your teammates, you run off like a crazy man after this stranger—leaving the goal wide open. The last thing you see behind you is Ahmad the Muslim scoring. It vaguely crosses your mind that the score is now 2–2. Ahmad is gloating and your teammates are glaring.

But you don't care. You've lost it. Gone off the rails. Fallen off your rocker. And you don't even know why or what for. You catch up with the man, who is now off the field and walking into the parking lot. He has attracted a small crowd by now, probably due to his strange attire and bizarre actions.

You're out of breath but manage to blurt, "Who are you and what do you want?"

"Come and see. Follow me," he replies.

What? Come and see? you think. *Who does he think he is?*

"But, sir," you gasp in exasperation, trying to be polite, "I can't just leave the game to follow someone I don't know. I have responsibilities."

Something dawns on you. You realize he doesn't seem concerned in the least about your soccer game. Which is strange since *everyone* is either on one team or the other.

"Okay, here's the deal," you nearly yell. "I'd follow you to wherever it is you're going if you'd at least tell me which side of the match you're on."

"Neither."

"Well, it can't be 'neither,' you have to be on one side or the other!" you exclaim.

"Neither," he repeats.

Again you tell him that's not possible as *everyone* is on one team or the other. "So which side are you on then? Your own?" you ask with sarcasm.

"Yep."

"So ... then, what's the name of your side?"

"Joshua. And if you'll stop asking questions and follow me you'll find out what I mean."

You're totally confused, but you do—follow him that is.

As you follow, you begin to learn that this soccer game you've been playing—that *everyone's* been playing—isn't the way. Joshua is. And that winning doesn't mean scoring more points than the other team. It's Joshua. *He's* the score. And all the strategies your team was using, though well meaning, really missed the whole point. You soon realize your life will never be the same following this Joshua guy.

What if I told you that this "us versus them" model of Christianity also misses the point? And that when you speak of Jesus from that paradigm, you are not only ineffective—you will also lose the game? Interested? Read on.

1

What's Missing in This Gospel?

I met Jesus when I was a little boy.

And then again when I was a teenager. And then again in college. And in YWAM (Youth With A Mission), too. And finally, when I moved to Beirut. We seemed to keep bumping into each other in this thing called *Christianity*. After running into Him for what seemed like the twentieth time, I invited Him to move in with me.

The problem was, after He moved in, He started throwing some of my stuff out, and I had pretty neat stuff. I had a college degree, I had a ministry, and I had a whole bunch of really valuable Christian things. Solid doctrines, good theology, and a vision for the lost.

And He threw them out.

I resorted to covert tactics. I would sneak out under the cover of darkness, wearing night-vision goggles and camouflage paint on my face, and I would rescue my valuables, hiding them in the garage where I could visit them when Jesus wasn't looking.

But He found them and threw them back out on the curb again, ready for the garbage truck to haul off like sacks of trash.

Why would Jesus throw out perfectly good doctrines and sound theology? I had worked *hard* for those things, and He tossed them out as if they had no value at all.

Maybe He knows something I don't.

I sometimes wonder, can somebody be "saved" and not even know it? Say a person meets Jesus and decides to follow Him, without having any concept of salvation, or heaven, or a moral code based on the wages of sin. What then?

What if our concept of salvation is based on a gospel that is the sum of its explainable parts? What if we consider ourselves "saved" because we have a dynamite explanation of *salvation?* We can correctly label and identify all the components. Sinners fallen away from God. God's mercy. Sacrifice for man's sins. The atonement. Justification by faith. Eternal life.

Let's try a litmus test: Try to describe your salvation using only the four Gospels, without using *any* of the above terms. You have one minute. *Go.*

I recently visited a missions school at a large church in Waco, Texas, and decided to try a similar test in a class-sized proportion.

"Tell me," I said to the group, "what is the gospel?"

A young lady raised her hand. "The free gift of God."

"Good," I said. I went to the chalkboard and wrote *gift from God*. "Somebody else?"

"Freedom from sin," a man near the back called out.

"Eternal life," said another.

"Keep going," I said. I stayed busy at the chalkboard, listing the items as they came in.

Freedom. Righteousness. Moral purity. Grace. Unconditional love. Healing and deliverance. Redemption. Faith in God. New life.

After five minutes or so, we had filled the chalkboard with a list of things that we believed were the gospel.

"Excellent," I said. "Did we miss anything?"

The room was silent for a minute. I could see heads turning. I could hear pages rustling. Everybody seemed to think there was something significant missing, but nobody wanted to volunteer to name the missing item.

Finally, after the second minute of silence, a girl near the front raised her hand. "How come none of us mentioned Jesus?"

"Exactly," I said. We closed the session and went to a break. Point made.

I've been reading Donald Miller's *Searching for God Knows What*. Miller took this point to an even further extreme. In his book, he tells a story about one occasion when he was speaking to a class at a Christian college. He stood in front of the group and announced he was going to share the gospel with them, with one difference: He was going to leave out one critical element. He warned them in advance that it was a major part and that he would require them to tell him what it was afterward. He went on to describe the rampant sin that plagued our culture: "homosexuality, abortion, drug use, song lyrics on the radio, newspaper headlines, and so on."[1] He said that, according to Scripture, the wages of sin is death, and he talked about the way sin separates us all from God.

He went on to describe "the beauty of morality," and told stories, citing examples of how righteous living was better. He spoke of the greatness of heaven, and described it complete with a landscape of spectacular beauty.

He talked about teen pregnancy, sexually transmitted diseases, and all the supporting statistics.

Finally he shared the caveat: repentance. How it would make life purposeful and pure and full of meaning, going into detail about "what it is they would be saved from if they would only repent, and how their lives could be God-honoring and God-centered."[2]

Describing what happened when he finished the lecture, Miller writes, "I rested my case and asked the class if they could tell me what it was I had left out of this gospel presentation."[3]

He waited for several awkward minutes. Not a single hand raised. No one could identify the missing component of the gospel. As far as the students could tell, Miller had been complete.

Closing his case, Miller writes, "I presented a gospel to Christian Bible college students and left out Jesus. *Nobody noticed,* even when I said I was going to neglect something very important, even when I asked them to think very hard about what it was … even when I stood there for several minutes in silence" (italics mine).[4]

Miller concludes: "To a culture that believes they 'go to heaven' based on whether or not they are morally pure, or that they understand some theological ideas, or that they are very spiritual, Jesus is completely unnecessary. At best, He is an after-thought, a technicality by which we become morally pure, or a subject of which we know, or a founding father of our woo-woo spirituality."[5]

I think that way often—more than I'd like to admit. Too often I try to win allies to my point of view rather than pointing to Jesus. I remember having lots of arguments with people of different perspectives. I exercised my tongue and my brain a lot in those situations. I fervently and (I hope) intelligently refuted arguments. I showed my mettle. I proved myself.

I proved that it was more important to me to win an argument than to be like Jesus—compassionate and loving. Kind and patient.

Twelve years in Lebanon broke the spine of the things I thought were important. You can only bang your head against a concrete wall for so long before it occurs to you, *It would hurt a lot less if I'd quit doing this.*

I am not sad to say that I was once a proud "missionary." I am grateful for the lessons I learned from that time of ignorance. Like many others, I learned loads when I tried to pound the square peg of Western politics/freedom/democracy/human rights into the round hole of a society a thousand (or more) years older than the one I came from.

The next time you get into an airport queue for a departure, look at the sign: You can only take one item as a carry-on. The rest goes into the storage of the aircraft.

This was the lesson I learned on the anvil of Beirut. You simply cannot change a person into your own likeness. It doesn't work. You cannot force-feed another person your perspective and expect it to stay down. As somebody once told me, "You have to realize every person is an I." Each individual has his/her own makeup. There is no way to download your beliefs into somebody else hoping they will take.

This reality is not exclusive to Muslims in Beirut. It is universal. No person, anywhere in the world, has a brain-port open to receive a personality change. There are only people like you and me. People with full brains and empty hearts. People who need Jesus, not a massive array of doctrine, polemics, and theology lessons. People who need a relationship. People who need to belong before they can believe.

We can only do one of two things: Give them Jesus or give them wasted sewage. We can either point the way to the Way or confuse them with a load of things that will never feed their need for God. There is a place for doctrines and dogma and science and history and apologetics, but these things are not Jesus—they are humanly manufactured attempts to make people think that having the right ideas is the same thing as loving and following Jesus.

Twenty years ago, I put my books in a box with my favorite football, packed my stuff away in storage, and went to Holland to join up with a missions base. I joined Youth With A Mission (YWAM—which we lovingly called Youth Without Any Money). My only claim to fame was that I led the small group that Floyd McClung Sr. and his wife attended. He was a minister of sizeable reputation, and I was a kid from the Midwest with soap still behind my ears.

We went on an outreach trip to Yemen, a coastal nation in the Persian Gulf, and it was like landing on another planet. The people were different, the language was bizarre, and there was sand everywhere. I mean *everywhere*. I would put on *clean* socks only to find an ounce of sand in the toe. We lived in tents. It was immersion treatment from day one, and it stuck to my soul. I was never the same.

When I returned home, I attended college in Colorado Springs, married the love of my life, and began to get involved with a Vineyard church in Denver. My heart beat with the same passion that infects so many today. *I wanted to change history.* I wanted to be there at the moment people became alive in Christ. I didn't fully understand what ministry was, but I dove in.

It was a lot different from what I imagined.

One day, my pastor, Steve, approached me with an offer. "Carl," he said, "I want you to lead a small group."

To which I promptly said, "*Lead?* Heck, no." Or something like that.

"I thought you wanted to be involved in our ministry," he said, surprised. "I've spoken to some of the others, and I've prayed about it. I think you'd do very well."

I took the task.

My wife, Chris, and I took charge of a small group. There were eight of us, and I jumped in with the most intensive teaching I could find. We studied, prayed, and persevered. For about a month.

Some churches and ministries advertise a success rate. You know, "the fastest growing church in Nebraska" or "the most powerful ministry in Denver." We were fast and powerful, all right. We went from eight people to two in a month. Put *that* on a brochure. It left Chris and me staring at each other with puzzled expressions asking, "What just happened?" I'll bet you can't exterminate an ant colony that fast.

Steve, the ever-optimistic pastor that he is, came up with a quick solution, rather like telling a fallen rodeo rider to cowboy up. "Carl, I've given it some thought, and I think you should do this again."

"Steve," I said, "I think you should double your medication." I didn't actually say that, but I did tell him he was crazy.

"Look," he said, "there's another group—the leaders want you to help them out, and you won't be alone."

I said no. But I did it anyway. We regrouped, cut our losses, and got back on the pony. In about a month, we had lost 80 percent of our new group, meaning Chris and I had to swap uncomfortable glances with the other leader and his wife.

As I said before, ministry was different from what I had imagined.

I remember thinking it was a good thing I wasn't in charge of something bigger. Picture me trying to get twelve disciples. I'd have to start with a hundred and fifty. Jesus started by Himself and changed the world. I could start with the world and end up by myself.

Once again, Steve told me to cowboy up and grouped Chris and me, with two others, into yet another, larger group with its existing leaders. Are we beginning to see a pattern here?

Of course, history saw the need to repeat itself, and when the group went under it left the six of us leaders trying to figure out what happened.

I happened. Welcome to the jungle.

Steve had a different tactic. "Carl, I want you to take charge of the homeless ministry."

"Great," I said, "at least they've got no place to go to."

"Come on," Steve said, "you can do this and you've got a great heart for the lost."

"Nope," I said.

I did it anyway.

In no time, the "ministry team" was down to Chris and me, and we were making sack lunches at night, enclosing an inspirational gospel card, and then getting up at oh-dark-thirty to deliver them to the lines of people at various relief offices in the metro area.

None of the homeless people ever darkened the doorstep of our church with our sack-lunch card in hand.

Score?

Ministry: 4. Carl: 0.

We worked the homeless ministry for months, but finally gave it up. I thought about calling myself Carl the Ministry Killer. I'd approached it with all the sincerity and energy I'd been able to muster, and came out with a flat zero score and more than a few negative feelings. I'm not the type to get depressed, but I had several dark moments, trying to grasp my vision for the lost in one hand while holding an unraveling rope in the other. I felt disowned by my own vision, but I prayed that a door would open somewhere, hoped to find a place I would be able to disciple people without driving them away.

Steve approached me once again. I tried to hide behind the furniture until he went away, but he found me, so I had to listen.

"Carl," he said, "there's a series of prisons down south, in Penrose and Cañon City. I'm putting you in charge of a prison outreach."

Brings new meaning to the phrase *captive audience,* doesn't it? I said, "I don't want to be responsible for a prison break or a riot," but, as we've all guessed, I ended up doing it anyway.

There were about thirty maximum-security inmates gathered in the forum, and I got up to speak, as scared as I'd ever been in my life. These were tough guys, serving some of the hardest time a federal court could give them. Some had committed unspeakable crimes. There would be no intimidating sermonizing from me, that was for sure.

So I went to square one and simply told them about Jesus. I had a quaking voice and quivering knees. I remember my voice faltered and I was sure everyone in the auditorium noticed.

Paul once wrote, "When I came to you, brothers, I did not come with eloquence or superior wisdom as I proclaimed to you the testimony about God. For I resolved to know nothing while I was with you except Jesus Christ and him crucified. I came to you in weakness and fear, and with much trembling" (1 Cor. 2:1–3).

As that phrase about fear and trembling crossed my mind, I found I could easily relate to Paul. I found the "decision" to be weak less voluntary. I trembled because there were murderers breathing the same air as *moi,* and one of my chief concerns was keeping Mrs. Medearis's husband in good health.

Miraculously, somehow the inmates and I connected. Honest— no bribery involved.

After a month of visiting the prison, our numbers did something I'd never seen before. They grew. The inmates were interested in Jesus, and we didn't even have to give away cigarettes.

For me, something deeper began. Although I wasn't fully aware of it at the time, the passage Paul wrote to the Corinthians burrowed down into my soul and cemented itself there.

It would be some time before that verse became the center of my life.

2

Unfair Advantage

About a year ago in Colorado Springs, a slightly humorous and possibly profound illustration of how we can focus on Jesus rather than our "Christianity" took place. I accepted an invitation to participate in a citywide discussion, hosted by a church, on the topic of interfaith dialogue. The church had already invited the local Catholic bishop, the leader of the local mosque and Islamic center, and two Jewish rabbis. They needed one more Muslim leader and one more Christian.

When they first contacted me, they asked if I knew another influential Muslim leader in the States and if I would be the other Christian guy in the panel.

The first question was simple. I knew plenty of good Muslim leaders who would love to do this and immediately thought of my imam friend from the Middle East who currently lived in the States.

The more complicated question was whether or not I'd represent "Christianity," given my propensity to focus on Jesus and leave the religious stuff to others. But the organizers knew me a bit and said it was okay if I just talked about Jesus and didn't worry about explaining or defending the doctrines of Christianity. So I agreed.

It was a funny night. Several hundred people crowded the hall as the introductions began. I sat at the far left end of the panel. On the other end were the two Muslims. In the middle were the two rabbis, then the bishop and me. The introductions went like this:

"The honorable Muslim sheikh, Imam Yusef el Ahmadi, leader of the Colorado Springs Islamic Society."

Next, "The doctor, sheikh, and leading thinker, Imam Ali bin Muhammad, president of the American Muslim Society of Imams"—and other really important things.

Then the two rabbis: "Rabbi Yossi Guren of the"—insert name of synagogue that sounds very important—and "the first woman rabbi in Colorado," founder and president of the most-amazing-something that I can't remember.

Finally, they introduced the bishop, a man immortalized as the Catholic leader of the Colorado Springs area since the beginning of time.

Then the host came to me and said—this is no lie—"And finally we have … uh …"

"Carl. The name's Carl," I said.

He was obviously embarrassed not to know my title or my great accomplishments—of which I have neither. So he just said, "Mr. Carl," and everyone laughed.

Each of us was supposed to answer two questions, and we each had three to five minutes to respond. The first question was, "How does your religion get you to heaven?"

Good question!

The two Muslim guys did a fine job articulating the various views within Islam on what it takes to get you to heaven, which all come down to the "will of God." The two Jewish rabbis did a great job explaining the uncertainty of life after death within Judaism, hence the focus on *this* life within their faith. The Catholic bishop also did a very good job helping everyone understand the various Christian interpretations of the afterlife and how to get there.

Then it was my turn. Believe me, I was praying for wisdom and something significant to say. This is what came out: "Actually, my religion doesn't get you to heaven."

I probably should have explained or added to that, but that's all I said. The other panelists shifted uncomfortably in their seats and the host asked if I'd like to explain a little more.

"Sure," I said. "It's just that I've never seen a religion save anyone. All religions are great at laying out some basic rules—dos and don'ts—that are good for our lives, but they don't really provide hope or any kind of eternal security. It seems religions end up causing more trouble than solving anything."

"So then," asked the host, "how do you get to heaven?"

This all seemed so basic, but I thought I might as well go ahead and state the obvious. "Well, it's Jesus. He didn't start a new religion. He came to provide us a model for life and a way to God. He's it. Believing in and following Him is the way. He takes us to heaven, not a religion."

On to simple question number two.

"How does your religion deal with terrorism?"

The two Muslims felt a little defensive about this question, but did a nice job denouncing all forms of terrorism and explaining how the Qur'an does not provide a place for it. The two Jewish rabbis spent most of their time trying to convince the two Muslims that they had misread their own book on the subject. The bishop gave a lovely talk about mercy mixed with justice.

Here's what I said:

"I don't really know. I'm not sure how the religion I grew up in would or should deal with terrorism. But I do have some thoughts how Jesus might deal with terrorists because He had two with Him in His inner circle of friends. A Zealot and a tax collector. A political insurgent and an economic terrorizer of the common folk. What He did with these two was bring them in as confidants. As students. Disciples. And made them apostles of the early faith. It actually seems to me that the worse someone was, the more Jesus liked them. He didn't just have 'mercy' in the way we think of it, as a sweet, sappy, lovey-dovey sort of thing. It was mercy with a bite. Mercy that led the people out of where they were into a new place. This is what Jesus did with the worst of His day. He was really only hard on one type of folks—people like us."

I looked down the line and smiled. "People like me. Hypocrites and such."

I'm sure at this point they were all wondering why they'd invited me. We did questions and answers for about twenty more minutes and then wrapped it up. Two things happened at the end of the night that made it all worthwhile.

I had a little crowd of people around me in the front asking questions. Some happy, others angry, and still others just slightly confused. One woman was more than a little upset with me. I'd obviously shaken up the box where she kept her faith and she needed to tell me a few things. Our conversation went something like this:

"You didn't even mention the Trinity!" she said.

"True," I replied, "but I didn't think I was talking about that and it didn't come up in the course of the conversation, so …"

That clearly wasn't good enough.

"But surely you do believe in the Trinity, don't you? And there are some other things you didn't mention as well that you should have, like the atonement."

I knew I needed to tread lightly with her. Everyone lives in a context and it's good to be sensitive to the American Christian context as much as any other. So I simply said, "You're probably right, and of course I believe everything that's in this book." I held up my Bible, showing her that it appeared well read.

Right then, a young man, hardly able to contain himself, blurted out, "I'm a Muslim. I came with the imam tonight. I'm from his mosque and he invited me to come." He turned and addressed the woman who had been speaking with me and said, "If this man had talked about theology or doctrine or even Christianity, I wouldn't have been interested. I've heard all of that from my Christian friends. But he talked about Jesus in a way I've never heard before and had never thought of. I thought it was amazing."

I looked at the woman, trying not to give her the "I told you so" stare. To her credit, she said, "Wow. Maybe you're right. I wonder if I've confused my religion with my Savior?"

At that moment the local imam—who had been engaged in plenty of interesting conversations at the other end of the stage—came up and said, "Carl, Carl, Carl. You had an unfair advantage." He was smiling but also wagging his finger in my face. I wasn't sure where this was going.

"What's that, sir?" I asked a little timidly.

"While we were all busy defending our religion and our positions, you simply talked about Jesus. You cheated!" Then he let out a huge laugh and slapped me on the back, said, "good job," and walked away.

I wonder if that sums it up. We have an unfair advantage. We know the Creator. We're friends with the King. We know where truth is found and its name. We know what brings life and what gives life and where eternal life resides. It's not fair. While others are explaining and defending various "isms" and "ologies," we're simply pointing people to our friend. The One who uncovers and disarms. The beginning and the end of the story.

I used to assume that all my problems reaching people with the good news came from the other side of the divide. I assumed my Muslim neighbors wouldn't know how to receive Christian faith. I assumed they were so alien and so spiritually incompetent that I would have to make up the difference. I would have to go even further to share the gospel, because *obviously* it wasn't working the way it was.

I now see the simple truth: I had the wrong message. I was giving the wrong gospel. I was so busy trying to convert people to

Christianity that Jesus never had a chance. I was clogging up His inroad with all kinds of modern, Western, and thoroughly socio-political ideas.

Obstructions to the gospel become more obvious when we attempt to share our faith with others. Based on my experience, at least 70 percent of witnessing encounters happen involuntarily. It's not *us* taking the gospel to *them*. It's *them* bringing the questions to *us*. And it's usually not a friendly meeting of the minds.

"How could you possibly believe in God?" people ask, as if it isn't remotely sensible to believe such a thing.

Have you ever been deliberately poked regarding your faith? If you happened to pick up this book and are still reading it—after scanning the cover and flipping through the pages for any sign of pictures—chances are good that at some point or another, somebody decided to prod you about your faith.

It could have been a neighbor leaning over the fence, discussing the weather, and then politics, and then, surprisingly, religion. Maybe a friend, a coworker, a student, or the person next to you in the checkout line at the supermarket. The questions and objections vary from the emotional "How could anybody be so stupid as to believe in …?" and "How could a loving God let my mother die?" all the way to the intellectually put "The facts simply don't acknowledge the existence of a God!"

Because we're "Christians," we unfortunately feel we have to own up to Christendom. We believe that we are responsible for the entire history of Christian faith and that it's our job to explain everything. Okay, so now it's on. You flush, feel the heat rising up your collar. The theology nerves in your brain and chest send out the emergency signals. Battle stations! Maybe you're indignant. Maybe you're intimidated. You're rushed, the possible arguments spring to your throat and ... and then what? Chances are, you fumble it. Or you make the person angry and defensive. Or even offensive.

When I was younger and still hammering my mind on the anvil of higher education, I had a professor who was a passionate atheist, and he loved to take Christianity to task for any reason. He was good at it too. In class, we'd discuss the Crusades, the church, the Reformation, and the negative effects of Christianity on the world. He would relentlessly accuse the church of disrupting or destroying native cultures with "Christian" standards. South America, the South Pacific islands, Africa, you name it. He was a proselytizer. He hoped to help the uninformed Christians find the light. It was intense, but it was one of my formative periods in life. It actually began to shape in my mind what was wrong with Christendom.

There'd be fifty students in his world history class, and easily half of us considered ourselves some type of Christian. We were prime targets. A strange ritual would begin: The room would almost physically change temperature. The air would thicken. The silence between declarations would speak with thunderous intensity. The professor would posture, pose questions, deliberate, and then level some withering conclusion at the establishment of Christianity. Christians. Us!

We would nudge each other, give sideways glances that asked, *Why don't you say something?*

What exactly were we supposed to say?

Professor: 1. Us: 0.

Not all such situations are antagonistic. Most of the time people are looking for answers, and even the angry ones are, in a sense, pleading. The plea is unique—more helplessness than cynicism. Sometimes it's a blunt statement, coming without pretext or warning. A desperate friend, a depressed acquaintance in a rare moment of honesty. Maybe even a complete stranger. But whoever they are, for whatever reason, they say, "My life sucks." Or something like that.

We think, *Your life sucks? How can you say it with such candor? So honestly? Is it desperation?* Can I even say *sucks* in a "Christian" book?

Is it our obvious virtue (laugh) that encourages these people to share, or just freak circumstance? We panic, we fumble, we falter, and we blurt out something weak. Or worse, anecdotal. Or we realize we don't have a clue what to say. The problem posed to so many of us is the blatant reality of the gospel itself. What is the gospel, how do we live it, and what do we share?

What's so discouraging about sharing your faith is that you tend to come away from it less sure than you went in. *Did I share the whole gospel? What did I miss? What if the person only heard a part of it and joins a weird cult?*

The nausea, the sweaty palms, the dizzy spells, the sweat dripping down your sides, ah yes. I call it a tender spot. During many occasions, I've done everything from freezing in the headlights to playing it cool. And all because I was never really sure what to say. Mostly, I had the wrong message. I felt I needed to clarify Christianity, answer for the Crusades, solve the problem of Original Sin, and defend the history of the church. What a weight!

So one minute you're minding your own business, and then *wham!* Somebody gives you the most important opportunity in the infinite cosmos: This person wants to know about … God. Talk about a tender spot. And *boink!* There it goes, a failed opportunity. An embarrassing moment. How could it go so wrong? The truth is on our side, isn't it?

Such a moment is painful because it makes us look inside. By causing us to look at ourselves, it causes self-doubt, which in turn results in despair. We look at the real condition of our lives; we briefly examine our satisfaction with Christianity, wonder why we're still struggling, and ask: *Why am I so sure, and, if I am so sure, I should easily be able to share with somebody else, right?* And with the resulting introspection, self-doubt, and despair, we can begin asking: *What do I believe? What is my faith? What is the message I believe—what is the gospel?*

I remember a similar occasion. Somebody said it to me: "My life sucks."

And I, being a gifted and intelligent believer, said, "Bummer."
Bummer?
That's it, bummer. I said, "bummer."

I can picture you reading this. You're probably laughing at me. You might even be slapping your forehead. Pathetic! A searching person just happens to wander my way, and I blow it with a "bummer"!

That's because, at the moment of truth, I realized I had to own up to all the human failure in the tapestry of Christendom. I was responsible for the sins of all the churches. I had to answer a miserable person and honestly tell them it's much nicer here inside.

"Bummer"?

Yeah, I know. Not exactly the wisdom of the ages.

I learned from it.

I realized my brain was working so hard thinking of ways to convert this guy to Christianity that I lost my unfair advantage.

His name is Jesus.

3

Owning Christianity

If we don't truly know what the gospel is, we have to find an explanation for Christianity. Rather than extending ourselves to the other person, we tend to defend our position. I think the majority of modern evangelism involves Christians trying to explain to everybody else why they believe what they believe because they're insecure themselves.

The line of thinking goes like this: *If we do a really good job, explain the message of salvation, offer some Scriptures, and then pull out the sinner's prayer, we'll make a convert.* In a way, we're drawing a line in the sand and telling people, "You're on that side, and you need to believe what I'm telling you in order to cross the line. Once you cross it, you're saved."

We should make a checklist.

"Do you confess that you're a sinner?"

Check.

"Do you know that the wages of sin is death?"

Check.

"Do you know that you need the free gift of God, the gift of salvation from sin?"

Check.

"Okay, repeat this prayer after me ..."

Check.

"Now what?"

"Now you're a Christian. Read this Bible every day and pray a lot. Try not to sin, because if you do you're taking advantage of God's grace and He doesn't like that very much, so He'll have to discipline you."

"Umm ... okay."

"By the way, welcome to the kingdom."

"Hey, wait a second, what did we just do?"

I admit it. If you're going to "make Christians" and "get people saved," it's not that easy. People are defensive about their flaws. If you walk into their lives on a five-minute tour, telling them everything they know is wrong and that unless they change their minds they could go to hell, of course they will put their guards up. As some people say, being "evangelized" can be like being sold a fire insurance policy.

In my experience, sharing Jesus is not all that difficult, even in a hostile environment. I don't tell people that they're sinning and that they're going to go to hell unless they believe what I believe. I just talk about Jesus. If, on the other hand, we believe that the gospel is a systematic explanation of Christianity, we have to own up to all the faults and failures of Christian history, while convincing people that Christianity really is better than whatever they believe.

Here's a few of the scenarios that "Christianity" brings to mind. The Irish Rebellion. The Protestants versus the Catholics. The religious genocides in Africa and the Balkans. What about the persecution of scientists like Copernicus and Galileo? What about the Inquisition? What about the Holocaust, slavery, and the modern white supremacy movement?

If you want to test this, simply ask natives of any continent what they think of when you say the word *Christian.* They could say anything. Crusader. Slave master. Warrior. They'll point to Cortez, de Gama, the armies of Constantine, and many others who came to the native lands, stole, ravaged, killed, and spread disease. All of these "Christians" came to ripe and plentiful lands and yanked the rug out from the indigenous people while forcing the "pagans" to convert, often at the tip of the sword or the muzzle of a musket.

When we preach Christianity, we find all these things on our plates. Trying to explain them moves the issue even further away from the gospel. We want to explain that Christianity is good at heart, but full of flawed and forgiven people. Sometimes this is effective. Usually not.

I believe that the gospel and the religion of Christianity can be two different messages. Even opposed on some points. When we preach Christianity, we have to own it. When we preach Jesus, we don't have to own anything. Jesus owns us. We don't have to defend

Him. We don't even have to explain Him. All we have to do is point with our fingers, like the blind man in the book of John, and say, "There is Jesus. All I know is that He touched me, and where I was once blind, now I see."

We have to open our eyes to the possibility that we're preaching the wrong message. We're busy trying to find the boundary line that separates the saved from the unsaved and trying to bring people across that boundary by convincing them to think like we do. Here in the West, reason is king. We have doctrines and apologetics and really nifty devices to solidify the right thoughts. If it doesn't make sense, it's not relevant.

How about that checklist from before?

"Do you think you're a sinner?"

"Yes, I think so. So-and-so told me I was."

"Do you think that the wages of sin is death?"

"Yep. The Bible says so."

Now I'm not saying those things are untrue. Yes, all have sinned and fallen far short of the kingdom of God. Yes, sin brings death as a natural consequence. And yes, Jesus was crucified to take our sin away from us. I don't deny these things. They're true. But we're wrong when we put our faith in our reason. We believe something because it makes sense to us; we grasp it with our reason, and we call that faith. We call that being saved. Thinking the right thoughts, knowing the right principles.

I don't want to redefine salvation. I don't want to redefine the gospel or even Christianity on the whole. I suppose I want to undefine them. I want to strip away the thousands of years of graffiti painted onto the gospel, turning it into a reasonable code of doctrines. The gospel is not an idea. It is not a belief. It is not a favorite verse. The gospel does not live in your church, it cannot be written down in a simple message, and it is not the sinner's prayer. The gospel is not a *what*. It is not a *how*. *The gospel is a Who*. The gospel is literally the good news of Jesus. *Jesus* is the gospel.

When I speak at different universities, one of my favorite things to do is to ask the students if they think I can give the history of Christianity in twenty minutes or less. Invariably, almost everybody thinks I can't. So I have somebody start a stopwatch, and I attempt to give the class the whole thing—all two thousand years of it—before the timer buzzes. Now, admittedly, this twenty-minute condensed version is very Western and very Protestant in its perspective, so please don't be offended if you're Catholic or an Easterner. I am also intentionally highlighting the negative aspects of our relgion to make a point. I suppose that even I have my bias.

AD 0–33: A Palestinian Jew named Jesus of Nazareth lived, taught, and demonstrated the coming of what He called the kingdom of God. He confronted the establishments, loved the sinners, healed the sick people, and then died as a sacrifice for the sins of all generations. Then He disappeared into the clouds, much to the disappointment of His followers.

AD 33¼: The Holy Spirit came with great power, and the disciples finally realized what the whole enchilada was about. (Just as Jesus promised, minus the word *enchilada*.)

AD 34–100: The original eleven disciples—plus Judas's replacement—along with about five hundred or so others, had some pretty radical years of fruitful ministry. They continued to teach what Jesus taught, along with stories of what He'd done. Mostly they stuck close to Israel, but then a new convert named Paul got his fingers in the pie and they started going to some exotic places: Turkey, Africa, Greece, and even north into Europe. It was a good-news-and-bad-news time. Many accepted this teaching of salvation and a new way to live; yet many also faced persecution, torture, and execution. Most of the followers died in nasty entertainment venues, like arenas where they were eaten by lions or forked by gladiators in front of thousands of cheering fans.

AD 100–313: The message of Jesus' kingdom spread through the Middle East, North Africa, Turkey, and Greece. Basically the whole Roman world. Followers of Jesus, Jew and Gentile alike, sprouted into communities. For every believer who was killed, ten more seemingly popped out of the ground to take his or her place. A few emperors and religious leaders apparently embraced this new concept of living life in relationship with the Creator, but many were repulsed by this growing demographic and its potential threat to the systems they had worked so hard to build.

During this period, people began to wander from the original teachings of Jesus. Hierarchies began to form. People gave themselves titles and positions. Rules and regulations began replacing the living daily relationship with the Spirit of God. A new religion called "Christianity" was born.

AD 313: The Roman emperor Constantine decided to make the religion of the Christians legal, and it later became the official religion of the expanding Western world. His decision was more political than personal, as Constantine continued to favor Mars and Apollo with his own offerings. That is, until one night in a dream he heard instructions to put the sign of the cross upon his soldiers' shields. After a victory, Constantine decided that the credit belonged to the God of the Christians and committed himself—at least in the public view—to the "Christian faith."

AD 313–1550: This new religion, Christianity, which was loosely based on the Bible and had very little to do with what Jesus said or did, expanded everywhere. Emperors and kings became religious dictators, killing any dissenters, forcing arbitrary conversion on people, clamping a title on them for the sake of political unity or military conscription. Somewhere within this time frame, people began to take the Greek word *ekklesia* and use it as a place-name noun: "the church."

Emperor Charlemagne, the founder of the Frankish Empire, invaded, defeated, and "Christianized" the territory he took, forcing Catholicism on the people, slaughtering those who refused. When he eventually settled down to rule his kingdom, he divided it into 350 counties. In order to maintain the loyalty of his subjects, he appointed *missi dominici,* or "emissaries of the Lord," to each of these territories to oversee the "spiritual condition" of the people, meaning of course that those with different viewpoints could be charged with "sin." His strategy kept the people in line politically using a supposedly spiritual entity—all in the name of Christ.

During this time, every few years, one radical preacher or another would get a hold on a pulpit and use his fifteen minutes of fame to call the people back to the teachings of Jesus. Usually these figures faced excommunication or death for their pains. Many who didn't die moved to the hinterlands to build places of retreat, typically called monasteries.

The Renaissance, which occurred near the end of this period, was similar in its inception to Christianity in that it got some things right. The thinking of this period arose from appreciating the dignity of humanity, the discoveries of science and nature, and the capacity of the mind and talents God gave humans. Good stuff. But generally speaking, people were confused about who was worshipping what. Some supported the papacy, others the monks, and still others adhered to various strains of deism, agnosticism, and in some cases, outright atheism.

Then, in 1517, a Catholic priest by the name of Martin Luther entered the scene. He realized that this thing called Christianity was a big mess and in need of an overhaul. So he wrote a list of ninety-five things that should be fixed. Guess what? Nobody appreciated it. Well, almost nobody. See, in the same way that Jesus didn't found the religion of Christianity, Luther didn't found the Protestant faith. He didn't want a new religion. He wanted to see some things changed within the Catholic system so he could conscientiously remain in it. Luther's attempt to urge reform never came to a satisfactory conclusion, and a resulting European and even pan-American theater of theology began. Before you knew it, Luther, Calvin, Zwingli, and later, Knox, were conversing over the precise definitions of words people like you and me can't even pronounce.

AD 1700: The period known as the Enlightenment arrived. While essentially the natural progression of men looking for more stuff to call their own, in some ways it continued where the Renaissance left off. People placed humanity at the center of the universe and put renewed emphasis on the power of the mind. In fact, people liked themselves so much that they practically built whole nations out of ideologies. The "individual" was supreme—giving rise to the idea of "individual human rights," a concept never conceived before. The later developments of representative government, religious freedom, and civil rights resulted from the thinking of the Enlightenment philosophers during this period.

AD 1800: The West expanded farther west, deeply south, and even to the Far East, conquering with the assistance of technology produced by the so-called Enlightenment. God, gold, and glory dominated the period.

From 1550 to 1850, the religion of Christianity divided and split into many different brand names. The original protesters had since dispersed into hundreds of types of Protestants. In fact, Protestantism seemed to thrive in the newly individualistic Western world. Building on the themes of the Renaissance and the Enlightenment came naturally for Westerners. They considered it an obligation to carry the gospel with them to the New World, zealously converting the natives to Christianity.

They were not all greedy and entrepreneurially driven men. A number of priests and missionaries went attempting to counterbalance these mercenary ventures by legitimately spreading the good news of Jesus among the newly oppressed natives. It is a mistake to paint these times with a wide brush of doubt. We can be sure, both through historical perspectives and firsthand accounts, that men of the cloth did honestly share the truth of Jesus in spite of the invasions they may have been part of, but were never party to.

Of course, in this era as in all the others before, voices in the wilderness called people to turn back. However, nobody really knew what they would be turning back to in the first place.

AD 1850–1900: This was the time of the thinkers Sigmund Freud, Karl Marx, Charles Darwin, and Friedrich Nietzsche. Four brilliant, edgy, ahead-of-their-time philosophers. Each one, in his own way, summarized "religion" as the easy way out for weaklings. Humankind was the answer. They asserted that we must be our own saviors, and that the answer is in economics, psychology, science, and philosophy.

This is very difficult for us to accept, but they may have been dead-on regarding the first point. What if religion really is a crutch? A crock? Something foolish people invent so that they can feel purpose or peace about their own existences?

The twentieth century: From about 1920 to the present day, the religion of Christianity has experienced a significant awakening. Fundamentalism, Pentecostalism, evangelicalism, and the various renewal groups have all but redefined what it means to be a "Christian." These groups tend to be Bible centered and worship oriented. Some are "Spirit filled." There's even been a gradual return to talking directly about Jesus again. But still, we have some scary questions to ponder.

We need to ask ourselves: What influence have all the different eras, philosophers, governments, and histories had on this thing we call "Christianity"? Is the modern system really built on the life and teachings of Jesus of Nazareth, or is it a complicated conglomeration of ideas and flaws from different centuries and different perspectives? Where did Jesus go in the bigger picture?

As I look over the history of Christendom, I notice our minds are where our hearts should be. The kingdom of Jesus has somehow become a religion of the mind rather than a spiritual response of the heart. We focus on psychological compliance rather than spiritual dependence upon the teachings of Jesus and the guidance of the Comforter, the Holy Spirit.

In the 1920s a missionary named E. Stanley Jones traveled to India to bring the gospel to the Hindus, the Muslims, and the Buddhists who lived there. He found himself standing in line behind Moses and David, Jesus and Paul, and Western civilization and the Christian church. He wrote, "I was worried. There was no well-defined issue. I found the battle almost invariably being pitched at one of these three places: the Old Testament, or Western Civilization, or the Christian Church. I had the ill-defined but instinctive feeling that the heart of the matter was being left out. Then I saw that I could, and should, shorten my line, that I could take my stand at Christ and before that non-Christian world refuse to know anything save Jesus Christ and him crucified."[1]

Does that sound familiar?

E. Stanley Jones continues this thought in his book *The Christ of the Indian Road:* "The sheer storm and stress of things had driven me to a place that I could hold. Then I saw that there is where I should have been all the time. I saw that the gospel lies in the person of Jesus, that he himself is the Good News, that my one task was to live and to present him. My task was simplified."[2]

What if we were to take Jesus at His word—"I, if I am lifted up from the earth, will draw all peoples to Myself" (John 12:32 NKJV)? What if our complicated explanations are wrong, not because they are incorrect, but because they do not constitute the person of Jesus?

Jones continues, "I found that when I was at the place of Jesus I was every moment upon the vital. Here at this place all the questions in heaven and earth were being settled. He was the one question that settled all others."[3]

When I struggled in Lebanon, the words of E. Stanley Jones struck me with profound and simple truth. The gospel is not a debate or a list of things to believe. The gospel is a person. Jesus Christ is the gospel. He is the truth. He is the point. He embodies all of the salvation/redemption/forgiveness/freedom stuff Himself, and because He is a personality, He does not require doctrinal mastery to connect with an individual.

In *Blue Like Jazz,* Donald Miller takes it one step further. He writes about a radio interview he had with a non-Christian talk show host who urged him to defend Christianity. Miller refused to do so, which made the host curious:

> He asked me if I was a Christian, and I told him yes. "Then why don't you want to defend Christianity?" he asked, confused. I told him I no longer knew what the term meant. Of the hundreds of thousands of people listening to his show that day, some of them had terrible experiences with Christianity; they may have been yelled at by a teacher in a Christian school, abused by a minister, or browbeaten by a Christian parent. To them, the term Christianity meant something that no Christian I know would defend. By fortifying the term, I am only making them more and more

angry. I won't do it. Stop ten people on the street and ask them what they think of when they hear the word Christianity, and they will give you ten different answers. How can I defend a term that means ten different things to ten different people? I told the radio show host that I would rather talk about Jesus, and how I came to believe that Jesus exists and that he likes me. The host looked back at me with tears in his eyes. When we were done, he asked if we could go get lunch together. He told me how much he didn't like Christianity but how he had always wanted to believe Jesus was the Son of God.[4]

Miller touches on a point that few of us would like to address publicly: the ambiguity of the word *Christian*. It is epidemically obvious that the word itself carries certain meanings, intentions, and misdirections. If you feel inclined to test this, try asking people at four or five different venues what they believe about Christians. Then consider: Would Jesus deny these differently impressed individuals an opportunity to follow Him?

One day I saw my Muslim-Arab friend sweating as he talked with my other friend, a fine, conservative-minded evangelical Christian.

It looked like the two had locked horns in a battle to the death. It happened here in Colorado this past summer. We hosted a gathering of some of our longtime friends from the Middle East and brought in a bunch of American Christian friends to talk about God, the Middle East, and how to bring hope to Muslim countries. There were about forty-five of us together for three days. We were having a great time—until I looked over and saw these two all tangled up.

The next thing I knew, my Muslim friend (not yet a follower of Jesus) had gone out on the deck and was smoking a cigarette like his life depended on how fast he could suck it down. I walked out and nonchalantly said, "What's up, bro?"

His response: "Why the $%&^@ do these people want to convert me? Why can't they just leave me alone? I know that *you* don't want to convert me. Right?"

Talk about a loaded question full of semantic nuance. Here's my answer and what happened.

I asked him what he thought my other friend wanted to convert him to. He said, "He wants me to be a Christian, but I'm a Muslim." I asked him what he thought this friend meant by becoming a Christian.

"He wants me to stop living in the Middle East and loving my family." I told him I was pretty sure that's not what this friend meant, but if that's what "conversion to Christianity" is, then I agreed—he shouldn't convert.

"*See,*" he said to me, "I knew you weren't into conversion."

"No I'm not," I said. "Not like that. Not at all. I think you should stay in your country, love your family, and be who God has made you to be."

Then I asked him this: "What do you think God thinks when He looks down at all 6.5 billion people on earth?"

"He thinks they're all screwed up," he said.

"Yep, that's what I think God's thinking too. So what do you think God would like to do with all these messed-up people? Muslims, Christians, Jews, Hindus, nothings, everyone?"

He had never thought of that before, so he wasn't sure. But he did say God would probably want to "help them not be so screwed up." I agreed.

"So you might say that God would like to convert all 6.5 billion people on earth. Not to a religion, but to Himself. He would like everyone to be like Him. To be converted into Him. But how would He do that? He'd need a converter."

I went on to tell my friend that if he bought an appliance here in the States and took it back to the Middle East, he'd need something to change the current from 110 to 220 volts. "What's that called?" I asked him.

"A transformer or converter," he said.

"That's right. So what is God's transformer to get us all back the way God wants us to be? To change us? To convert us?"

He gasped (literally) and said, "It's Jesus. I never thought of that—but it's Jesus. He's the converter."

He got so excited he called his wife out and told her the whole conversation. She started to cry.

We sat on the deck and prayed that God's "converter" or "transformer" would change us into the current that can be connected to God. And that He would do this with all of our friends.

It was a profound moment. Amazing that just a half hour earlier he was about to bite this other guy's head off for "trying to convert" him and now he sat with me in tears praying.

The power of words.

Pretend you're handcuffed to something. The cuffs circle your wrists, and the links of chain lace through the bars of a rocking chair. Laughable, isn't it? I mean, who gets cuffed to a rocking chair? As funny as it is, you'd have to admit that it would be difficult to do much of anything while fastened to a piece of furniture. Except maybe rock in the chair. Try taking a shower with a rocking chair. Or going out to check the mail. Or even drinking a cup of coffee.

You'd be almost completely ineffective. In fact, you'd become a nuisance. The clattering and clunking would be like a cowbell. People would raise their eyebrows, sigh, and let you clunk right up to them. "Hi, guys," you'd pant, breathless. "What's up?" They'd look at each other, pretending not to see your rocking chair. And then they'd have to decide whether or not to mention your predicament, given the obvious embarrassment of it.

When we approach people and say, "Let me tell you how you can be saved," why is it like dragging a rocking chair and wearing a clown hat? Because there are big and awkward objects chained to the gospel. Why is it so painful and embarrassing to share our faith? Because the gospel has become encumbered, handcuffed to traditions, movements, and organizations. Even handcuffed to society and government. To millions of people around the world, Jesus Christ is synonymous with Western society and America.

The problem isn't that these attachments are or aren't good; the problem is that these things are not the gospel. Do we really want to try to redefine and reinterpret Jesus and then give Him to the world? Of course not. When we handcuff things to Jesus, we are convoluting the message. The power of Jesus' life and death come from His existence as the exact representation of His Father. Do we really want to add to that?

4

In or Out

Draw a circle on a sheet of paper. Or breathe on the mirror and make a circle in the fog. Inside the circle, make little dots and give them names. These dots represent the people whom you consider solid Christians. Maybe you're one of them. On the outside of the circle, make some other dots. These dots are the ones whom you know are not solid Christians. They drink/smoke/cuss and maybe even kick their dogs. This diagram represents the idea of salvation many of us have. We live in the circle and, to bring others inside of it, we have to convince them to adopt our beliefs. We typically use the word *confession* to describe the act when someone self-narrates his or her change of heart.

So we pick up our megaphones and we tell the people outside of the circle about God. And some of them are interested.

"Yoo-hoo!" we shout. "Over here, in the circle!"

They come closer, curious. "Hey," they say, "what are you guys shouting about?"

"We're glad you asked," we say. "We're Christians, and we want you to be one also!"

Some of them leave, so we turn up the volume on our megaphones. "*Hey!*" we shout. "*Don't go—we really have good news in here!*"

A few of them stick around, and so we point to the circle, the line in the ground, the boundary we believe makes us different from them. "This line," we say, "is very important. We have eternal life, and you don't. And that is a bad thing."

The people outside the circle look at each other. "Do you guys have a secret code language or something? You're not making any sense."

"Yes we are!" we say. "Wait, don't go!"

A few more people drift away. Now there's only two people left, and they look uncomfortable, shuffling their feet and looking down. "What do we have to do to get eternal life?" one of them asks.

"You have to come inside the circle," we say.

"How do we do that?" they ask.

"We're experts," we say. "It's why we're here. To rescue you guys from the world."

One of them throws her hands in the air and says, "I don't need to be rescued. See you later." And she goes away.

Now there's the one guy left, and since he's Last Man Standing, he decides he may as well commit. "Count me in," he says. "What do I have to do?"

"First you have to pray this prayer, and you have to quit sinning, okay?"

"Okay." He folds his hands and bows his head, awkwardly but sincerely.

We pray the prayer together, and a few of us imagine that angels are cartwheeling around the halls of heaven in ecstasy, shouting, "We got another one!"

"So," says Last Man Standing, "what's this sinning I'm supposed to quit?" He pulls out a cigarette, lights it, and takes a long drag.

We cough and pinch our noses. "Well—it might be a good idea if you put that out."

"Oh, sorry, don't smoke?" he says.

"No, but that's not really the issue," we say, nodding in agreement with each other. "But let's not get into that right now. We need to make sure that you know what you believe, now that you're a Christian and all, because that's what's important: knowing what you believe."

He stubs out his smoke, sits down, and opens his ears. "What's first?"

"Well," I say, "you need the Holy Spirit to come into your life. We call this being 'Spirit filled.'"

He frowns.

Somebody interrupts me. "Wait a second—that's not right! He has to be baptized first. Let's find some water."

"Okay," I say. We get up and start looking for some water.

Last Man Standing is now confused. "What do we need water for?"

"You need to make a public display of your faith in God, and you have to be dipped in water."

"Or sprinkled," interjects somebody else.

"Immersion is the only baptism in the New Testament," the first guy retorts, "and you need to reread the Bible."

"Guys! Come on, it doesn't matter!" I shout.

"Yeah," somebody agrees, "we just need to baptize him in the name of the Father, the Son, and the Holy Ghost."

"What?" Last Man Standing starts to edge away from the border of the circle. "I thought you were telling me about one God. Now you're saying that there's three of them?"

"No," I say.

"Yes!" somebody else says at the same time. We look at each other and our eyes widen. There's an awkward pause. Somebody has to explain it. Finally, I shrug. "Okay, I'll explain it."

"Explain what?" asks Last Man Standing, reaching for his smokes again, looking insecure.

"The Trinity," I say with a sigh. "You see, God is like … an egg."

Okay, stop. Parody aside. Let's address this.

The thirsty sinner comes and on bended knee says, "God, I'm thirsty."

And sometimes—let's be honest—we give them a drink from a fire hose. Of course we don't intend to confuse, and I'm not trying to make Christians seem like confusing people. We don't intend to be. But the question invariably comes up: "What do I have to believe now?"

What are we supposed to say? I remember trying to explain the word *sacrifice* to a teenage boy at an outreach. He'd asked me about Jesus being a sacrifice, so I attempted to explain the entire history of Levitical sacrifices for sins, because I hoped he would understand the concept of Jesus sacrificing Himself for the faults of sinful people. I lost him at the word *altar.*

"Man," he said, "you may as well be speaking Greek to me."

"Actually," I said, "the children of Israel spoke Hebrew."

I could slap my forehead now, just thinking about it.

But it's not just the difference in linguistics. When we stand inside the circle, trying to get people "into the kingdom," we mistakenly do two things wrong. First, we try to "download" the right definitions, doctrines, and beliefs into the brains of people who don't know the apostle Peter from Homer Simpson. By doing that, we communicate that having the right thoughts is the means of salvation. We're telling them that it's the stuff that happens between their ears that matters. When we focus on ideology, we're not touching thirsty hearts. Thirsty people don't want to memorize theology any more than they want to learn a new language.

Second, we're taking God's job out of His very capable hands. When we point at the boundary, we're trying to define it. But if Jesus is lifted up, *He* draws people to Himself. It isn't our job to lose sleep trying to decide if so-and-so is "in" or "out." If we were to look at Jesus, in the totality of His love and determination, we would realize we are not required to make ourselves His followers by force of reason. We would realize He came to us in *our* poverty of mind and heart. It is our job to follow Jesus, like Paul and E. Stanley Jones, refusing to know anything else but the crucified and resurrected Jesus.

Remembering the last exercise, instead of a circle, make a dot in the middle of the page. This is the Jesus dot. Sprinkle the rest of the page with dots. Find a dot that has the appropriate distance from the Jesus dot and put your name above it. Find another dot, a dot really close to the Jesus dot, and name it "Carl Medearis." Just kidding. I wanted to see if you were reading or skimming. Anyway, instead of measuring the distance between you and Jesus, make a little arrow from the dot, and point it toward Jesus. You're following Jesus. Find another dot, somebody you know is trying to follow Jesus too. Make another little arrow. Continue.

As you go, you'll notice a pattern of attraction. Instead of a theologically manufactured, doctrinally approved boundary, there is only the space between the person and Jesus. The differential is the arrow, which designates the intention of the heart. As Jesus Himself pointed out, this arrow is often guided by bare need. Sinners are often aware of this need, and the arrow points accordingly. It is interesting to note that morally "superior" people are often lacking the arrow of those who are much more sinful and much more needy.

Let's take a different approach. Jesus, as a person, is interesting to many. I don't mean solely as an object of abstract scrutiny. Now, some of the dots may not know Jesus or care to. Maybe their arrows point away from Him. Maybe you know a Hindu holy man or a devout Buddhist. The arrow may not point at Jesus, but obviously the little dot is seeking something, looking for some meaning, so you could draw a little squiggly, ambiguously pointed arrow.

When you're done with the sheet, step back and stare at it.

Whoa … it's a bit scary, isn't it? There's no line! There's no line telling you whether you are in or out. Maybe your devout Baptist neighbor is ahead of you! Maybe I'm not as close as you are! What are we to do?

I call this salvation insecurity. My friend Phil calls it control-freak Christianity. We want to measure, define, scrutinize, and secure our place on the "inside." And then, with that template in place, we go out into all the world to make other people nervous about whether or not they're in the circle.

I admit the arrow approach is a massive paradigm shift. Maybe on Sunday you feel close to the Jesus dot. Monday might be different. What to do?

Here's what I'm *not* saying. I'm not advocating either the "once saved, always saved" doctrine or the "salvation by works" doctrine. I'm not advocating any doctrine. I'm not claiming that it's all relative and you just have to be kind of good when you can and if you want to. And I'm not saying there isn't a point at which people genuinely come into the kingdom. Jesus preached this. He said, "I am the way and the truth and the life. No one comes to the Father except through me" (John 14:6). He wasn't negotiating. He is the personality and exact representation of God. And there simply isn't another way to get "in" besides Jesus.

Now draw a new dot on the center of a fresh sheet. This is still the Jesus dot. Draw a smattering of dots around it. Pick two that are a sizeable distance away and name them Peter and Andrew.

One day, Jesus was walking by the Sea of Galilee. He wasn't a major figure yet in terms of society. He was actually unknown, walking everywhere, interjecting Himself into people's lives, and saying, "Change your hearts, because the kingdom of God is here." Anyway, He walked by a pair of brothers throwing their fishing nets into the water and dragging the load back into the boat.

Jesus stopped where they could see Him and said simply, "Follow Me, and I will make you fishers of men" (Matt. 4:19 NKJV).

He didn't hunker down in the dirt and draw a circle with a stick and say, "See this dot here, this is Me. These two dots way out here are you guys. We're going to work on that."

He said, "Follow Me." It doesn't get much more basic than that, does it? So who decides the "if" and "when" of Peter and Andrew's salvation? Does it matter? Matthew says that "at once they left their nets and followed him" (Matt. 4:20). Without receiving an adequate explanation.

The distance between people and Jesus isn't doctrinal. It isn't political or social or even theological. It's a matter of personal contact. Jesus collided with two fishermen, and their lives were changed. In fact, the world was changed.

Never once, in all of recorded Scripture, did Jesus sit down to ratify or charter a basic "kingdom outline" so we could measure and compare ourselves and our friends against the boundary. Not even once. That's because Jesus is, in Himself, the gospel. Once He makes contact, our hearts struggle within us, and we, like Peter and Andrew, have to choose to follow or not. Jesus says, "I am the way." Why do we read this to mean Jesus *knows* the way or Jesus *shows* the way?

We don't trust *Jesus* with our salvation. We think He needs our help. We think He needs our doctrines, our church charters, our definitions, and our circle. We're insecure about our salvation, and we try to cement ourselves into security by surrounding ourselves with all the right stuff. We have the right doctrinal beliefs. We have the right philosophy. We're in the kingdom, and we can prove it.

Throw the circle away! It's okay to be a dot without a perceived circle for comfort. Remember, Jesus is the Way, and He started by saying, "Follow Me."

If all of this gives you pause, then I suggest a thought. We do not really know the gospel. It's part of a multifaceted tapestry of other things. We have misplaced the gospel, perhaps become blind to it. It has become hidden in sermons, churches, self-help books, and apologetic philosophies.

I know that it can be difficult to differentiate between good theology and Jesus because in our culture they are glued together. To us, Jesus evolved from an ancient culture into a modern, churchgoing, legalistic, politically active, conservative Westerner. We see Jesus through the lenses of our concerns and grievances. We think of Jesus as an evangelical Christian.

I often have to force myself to come back to the straightforward resolution of Paul: to simply know nothing else but Jesus. I know the one place I can't go wrong is the place where Jesus is. I can be weak, sinful, foolish, and even rebellious. I can fail others, ruin ministries, fumble my work, and still, I cannot go wrong when I stand with fear and trembling, knowing only Jesus Christ.

Often, instead of actually following Jesus, we're trying to do all the things Christianity tells us, hoping to come out in the same place as Jesus. We have the right goal, but we're following the wrong guide. I realize that it offends many people when I say that Jesus and Christianity are not the same thing. I've even heard it said that Christianity is the living Jesus on earth now. "John 1:1 says that Jesus is the Word," someone admonished me, "and that clearly means if we're living according to the Word, then we're being Jesus."

The problem here is one that I can't solve. It's a simple fact that there are complexities in both the world and the Bible. As Donald Miller pointed out, Christianity means ten different things to ten different people.[1] That's why I propose that we simplify all of the explanation and doctrine down to the pure nucleus: the person of Jesus Christ.

I'm not a brilliant theologian. I could preach endless sermons and write numerous books and never say any of this stuff exactly right. Let's simplify by making two generalized distinctions. For the duration of this book, I'll use *Christianity* as the catchall term for the Western model. Western Christian history, doctrine, theology, Western-style churches, reason, dogma, and denominations are all products and parts of Christianity.

The second distinction: What I'm proposing is simply following *Jesus*. This means learning from Him, obeying His teaching, doing what He did. Instead of trying to define the line that separates the saved from the unsaved, we point to Jesus. We don't have to "own up to" Christendom this way. We simply follow Jesus.

Christianity is problematic in so many ways. While the ideals of Christianity have a basis in Jesus, in the history of the world—from the Crusades to Calvin's oppression of Geneva—we have often seen everything but Jesus' love. Culturally, Christianity has met with resistance because of this pained history, and also because, to most of the world, embracing Christianity means embracing Western civilization, Western policy, and even Western rule.

Even within the boundaries of our own "civilized" countries, we can see the systemic problems within Christianity. Picketers, political manipulators, and cultural warmongers all tend to have their own versions of Christianity. Many racists consider themselves Christians. The same goes for many corrupt politicians, gangsters, and abusive parents.

The coin has another side too. Within the domain of Christianity, we all suffer beneath the weight of sin. Understanding the doctrine of forgiveness does not deliver us from sin. Jesus does. Our Western logic, our reason, our "right thinking" cannot deliver us from evil.

John, known as "the disciple whom Jesus loved," wrote, "For the law was given through Moses; grace and truth came through Jesus Christ" (John 1:17). Rather than maintaining his Jewish allegiance to the laws of Moses, he chose to live in the grace of Jesus, taking the truth of Jesus' love as his foremost identity.

As Christians, we're faced with a problem difficult to see because it's so obvious. We're aware of Jesus, but we are obsessed with Christianity. We're stuck on its requirements and we're defined by its doctrines, caught in an endless struggle to find out where we fit, if we've "arrived" yet, and if we're doing it right. We struggle with sin, and yet, because of the boundaries, we're forced to decide between being honest about our feelings and hiding for fear we'll be judged. In this state, we're not living in the grace of Jesus. We're trying to maintain our membership.

With Christianity, there's always the question "am I good enough?" Whereas Jesus announced that He was present for those who needed Him, as a physician for the ill and wounded, within the church, we often feel the need to conform—to fit all of life's questions and struggles into a system of answers. We all know how convoluted this becomes on the personal level. As Christians, we learn to take our struggles and "baptize" them with spiritual phrases. The root problems don't go away, they just vanish behind smoke and mirrors so we can get on with it. This is like taking aspirin for brain cancer.

It boils down to how we see our salvation. If we're saved into the boundaries of a circle, we owe our allegiance to that boundary, and we're going to try to bring others inside it. Theologian Dallas Willard calls this "bar code faith." He writes:

> The theology of Christian trinkets says there is something about the Christian that works like the bar code. Some ritual, some belief, or some association with a group affect God the way the bar code affects the scanner. Perhaps there occurred a moment of some mental assent to a creed, or an association entered into with a church. God "scans" it, and forgiveness floods forth. An appropriate amount of righteousness is shifted from Christ's account to our account in the bank of heaven, and all our debts are paid. We are, accordingly, "saved."[2]

Willard continues, "Many are distressed about this disjunction between faith and life, *but they remain firmly pinned to it by their ideas about salvation*" (italics mine).[3]

I know what I've said is very dangerous and will upset some. "Of course we know who's in and who's out," you say with a bit of panic in your voice. "Those who profess Jesus are 'in' and those who don't are 'out.'"

Just to provide a moment of relief for you, the reader, I do think that the Scriptures teach a fairly clear "in" and "out." There is a kingdom of light and a kingdom of darkness. In Christ and not in Christ. A wheat and a tare. A sheep and a goat. Lots of such analogies.

So since it's so clear, let me ask you some questions:

Does everyone who professes to know Christ actually know Him? (That's an easy one if you've read the Gospels.)

Does everyone who goes to church know Jesus? Also should be fairly easy.

Does everyone actually following Jesus call him or herself a Christian? (We've already tackled that one a bit, and you should know the answer.)

Okay, a little more difficult one: Does everyone who goes to a really good Bible-believing church and who could score ten out of ten on a doctrinal test know Jesus? If you came up with *no,* then we need to ask ourselves this: How *can* we know? Good question. How can we know who "we" are and who "they" are?

I think Jesus provides the answer when He says that we will know and be known by our fruit. And the one who obeys Him and does what He says has true faith. So ... it's by faith expressed in obedience to the will of God. But even that's not always so easy to see.

Maybe you'll read this and think that I'm trying to make salvation easier or make a way for all the gays and liberals and Muslims and Buddhists to get in without going through all the "proper channels."

Maybe yes and maybe no. I'm not trying to change what salvation is because salvation is not my responsibility. God didn't put Carl

Medearis in charge of deciding who stays and who goes. That's Jesus' job, and He can keep it.

My job, no—my *joy* comes from sharing the good news of Jesus with people. I point to Him, and He does all the heavy thinking. I don't have to convince anybody of anything.

I let Jesus run His kingdom.

5

What Would Paul Say?

I get this question a lot: "Jesus? Isn't He the guy who started Christianity?"

Close, but no cigar.

"Um, no, actually," I say, "that would be Constantine, or Pope Leo, or someone like that."

I usually get a blank stare in return.

What's remarkable about Jesus is what He didn't start. What He didn't do. Jesus didn't fix the world. He didn't solve its major maladies. As a matter of fact, He specifically avoided all titles and responsibilities that would have given Him political authority. Martin Luther believed that Jesus was so humble and low that "the devil overlooked him and did not recognize him."[1]

In the wilderness, hungry and alone, Jesus fought against not only the tempter, but also the temptation. Satan volunteered to surrender all the kingdoms of the world, if only Jesus would bow in worship. Talk about an opportunity for world peace! If Jesus could have fudged His ideals for a minute, He would have had the world at His feet. All His plans for the human race could have been realized with one minute's work. Yet Jesus refused the easy way.

I've often wondered why Jesus didn't just beat Satan right then and there. He could have. Why not? Show him who's the boss and then get on with the program. But He didn't. Why? According to the humanitarian ideal, Jesus fell far short. He didn't do as much as He could have.

But He started Christianity, right? Jesus, CEO.

Nope.

He started the church, right?

I don't know, which church? There's only twenty-five hundred or so denominations. Let's not even mention the differences between them. It begins to look like we're panhandling Jesus for His endorsement of our brand. Like He'd shoot a commercial for us. "Jesus, look at the camera, please." When we get to that point, we're way off. Jesus can't be stereotyped, categorized, or filed away. He doesn't fit in our filing cabinet.

When we go out into the world with our "Christian" message, we have to compete against thousands of other messages. We have to go toe-to-toe with asceticism, materialism, and belief in reincarnation. There are six billion people out there cramming everything they can into the lonely holes in their hearts, whether it's sensible or not. Whether it's logical or not. Whether it's deadly or not.

Like pained patients in hospital beds, they're mashing the morphine button as often as they can. Drugs, booze, pills, karma, new cars, new houses, new spouses. Christianity cannot compete with that. Christianity is a boundary telling all those pained people they have to give up their medication before we'll accept them. Before we'll love them.

But Jesus can go toe-to-toe with anything. There is no person in human history who holds a candle to Jesus. When we make sharing our faith a war of ideals, we create casualties on both sides of the boundary. We fight an "us versus them" campaign trying to show that our religion, our logic, our reason, our theology is better than everyone else's. After demolishing their beliefs, we try to rebuild a structure of proprietary mental acknowledgment. Think the right things, and you'll have the magical bar code the scanners of heaven will accept with a *beep.*

Did Jesus come into the world to build a new kingdom? Did He hope to found an organization that would end human suffering, create hope and peace? Did Jesus plant a church or even reach one city for God?

No.

Jesus didn't come to build a kingdom. He brought one with Him. He *is* the kingdom. He is the entry point to it. Look at the tense of Jesus' message: By saying "the kingdom of heaven is at hand" (Matt. 3:2 NKJV), He was saying that the kingdom of heaven is available now.

Because He spoke in the outlying regions, not from the pulpit of the temple, He spread this good news to people who were never likely to get within touching distance of an altar. "The kingdom of heaven is at hand," He would say. No doubt heads turned, whispers abounded. "Where? Do you see it?"

Wherever He went, the pained and lost people He met followed Him. Jesus' gospel was that *He* was the kingdom of heaven, with an easy and light yoke. He was available, and He was compassionate. And it appears that He was making house calls.

When we see His first encounter with the brothers Peter and Andrew, Jesus didn't hold a quick meeting to get His objectives out in the open. He didn't garner support or build a ministry team.

"Look, here's the plan," He could easily have said, "I came here to die as a sacrifice for the sins of all mankind. When I do that, we're going to build a church, and we're going to reach the lost. All you have to do is believe in Me."

When Jesus died, He was broke. His disciples split, His followers turned on Him, and He had to give His mother away to His friend John. Is it any wonder that Satan could overlook someone so low? All of the things that were high and lofty, all of the power brokers, all of the political offices and strategic objectives were far from this humble man, this Galilean who spoke about loving enemies and turning the other cheek.

I wonder: Do we overlook Him too?

Some amazing preachers, speakers, missionaries, and professors have emerged over the years. People who seem to have the singular qualification of being good at talking. They can pace the stage, pause behind the podium, and rivet the rest of us to our seats with a gaze. Due to the proliferation of good speakers, our message has become a little bit diluted. I admit, here I am on chapter five and I'm finding it difficult to keep the message focused on Jesus, and I've spent much of my time researching other speakers, writers, and thinkers.

Why do we do that?

Jesus is the message, isn't He?

Of course. But then, there are only a few dozen chapters written about Him in the entire Bible, compared to the major and minor prophets, the poetry books, the law, and the complete works of the apostle Paul.

I think Paul is the poster boy of the Western church. He single-handedly wrote the first great sermons, sermons we still hear today. He was a type A personality, a real go-getter, a champion church builder. He worked hard, suffered hard, and spoke with a sincerity and authority that has remained unrivaled to this day.

And here's what we love about him: He makes sense of the complex issues for us. He was an intellectual, a philosopher of the first degree. Two-thirds of the New Testament came from his mind, his heart. Paul had the unerring ability to dissect the mechanics of the kingdom of God and lay them out for the churches he built. He made sense of faith. He made sense of grace. He understood the exchange of God's love for us in our sins.

Today, in any Christian church in America, on any Sunday, you are likely to hear the words of Paul in a sermon. How we ought to live, how we ought to conduct our marriages, our businesses, our behavior. Love, money, charity, church structure, etc. These were Paul's areas of expertise.

But like some other heroes of the faith, Paul suffers from a case of mistaken identity. We've made Jesus and His messengers interchangeable. While all Scripture is from God and therefore important, do we believe that a message from Paul is as good as a message from Jesus? We studiously apply ourselves to Pauline doctrine. We struggle to live it the way we're exhorted to. At church last week I heard four passages of Scripture from a letter that Paul wrote, and only … zero words from Jesus.

What would Paul say? He didn't have a New Testament to preach out of. He had a blinding experience and a profound insight into the person of Jesus. No detailed notes. During his few encounters with the original disciples, Paul was up to his ears in conflict. Does that make Paul wrong? Of course not.

Perhaps we're drawn to the teachings of Paul because his change was so radical. Whereas he'd been a murderer, he became the victim of the very persecution he'd once led. Perhaps we're attracted to Paul because he looks successful, and we in the West worship success. I think this is ground zero for most Christians. We think that if it's not successful, it's not real. We think that if we don't succeed we're invalid. We don't count.

Paul went into some of the very worst pagan pits in the known world and left in his wake a series of growing churches and earnest followers. He is also one of the most widely read authors of all time. Maybe Paul reflects a kind of success that we in the West can relate to because we want so badly to succeed. This is ironic because, as time went on, Paul began to refer to himself more negatively. He went from calling himself an apostle to the very worst sinner ever. It's almost like he discovered more and more each day that his contribution to the world was insignificant. And yet in his core he realized that Jesus' contribution was more than enough.

This is not a case of Paul versus Jesus. They're not in any kind of doctrinal debate against each other. If Paul and you and I sat down today for a cup of coffee, Paul would talk about one thing above all. He would talk about Jesus. If Paul could make one exhortation to today's church, he might simply plead with it to stick close to Jesus.

Why do I say that? Because Paul loved Jesus. Because Paul was himself redeemed by the pure gospel—a burning light on a dusty road and a voice that struck him to the core. Above all, Paul understood that Jesus was of sole importance. Remember how he wrote to the church at Corinth, "I resolve to know nothing except Jesus"? He wasn't posturing so that he could follow with a great message. He was making an obvious and public declaration of his priorities. He was saying, "Get this: There is one thing that matters above all. Jesus Christ."

Paul isn't a mystery. His words aren't enigmatic. You always know where Paul stands on something. Flip to any page in the New Testament, and you'll more than likely find a passage that will tell you in concrete terms how you should conduct your life and what you should fasten your beliefs to. That was Paul's gift, and he fought for it until his death. He was truly a great man.

But he was only a messenger. He wasn't the message. He even said so, identifying himself both as a keeper of some kind of mystery and a "prisoner of Christ Jesus" (Eph. 3:1). Paul's gospel was never about himself. So why do we make it about him?

Many years ago, when I was with Youth With A Mission, I stopped one day in the middle of some homework and took stock of my surroundings. On the walls were plaques, signs, paintings, and posters declaring the YWAM objectives: Go and Do. Know God and Make Him Known.

YWAM has a thing for the Great Commission, which I think is terrific. As I looked around, though, I couldn't find anything directly from Jesus. Confused, I turned to the paper I was working on. It addressed the classic "Romans Road" method, leading from lost to saved to sanctified, just like that. But other than in second-hand references, Jesus did not appear. The theology was sound and well thought out, but Jesus was missing, except for a couple quotes from Paul and the all-time favorite: John 3:16.

I realized that I was telling people about something that someone else wrote about someone else once. I had to convince them that the Bible was 100 percent true before my message would stick. And even then, it would be my responsibility to make certain that Paul made sense of Jesus and that Jesus made sense at all.

I was putting Jesus in the fifth row.

Westerners are convinced that order is all-important. We tell people that they have to believe in God. Then we tell them that they have to believe that the Bible is God's Word. Then we have to convince them the Word says that they are sinners. Then we have to tell them Paul says that Jesus is the Way. We have to make sure Paul makes sense to them because Paul makes sense to us. We're making Paul the linchpin in the whole deal. I'm not sure he wanted that.

Is it critical that people "believe in God" before we tell them about Jesus? Didn't Jesus come here in the flesh to meet people who could not or would not acknowledge God in the first place? Must we filter the gospel through Paul's writings before we share our faith with others? Do we believe because Paul makes sense to us or because Jesus came to us and said something like "follow Me"?

Are we saved by our brains or our hearts?

Is there something wrong with pointing to Jesus in the first place, so that He can do the explaining? Do we trust God with salvation? There are some of you who will read this and become upset. You'll accuse me of taking a scalpel to the New Testament. Not so. Everything in the Bible is there for a divine purpose. I won't pretend to know it all. I'm not the Bible Answer Man. I like the fact that it's mysterious.

I don't know all the doctrine. I don't know about all the spiritual gifts. I don't pray as much as I should or read three chapters of the Bible every day. I don't feel confident and secure in my faith all the time. But I do know one thing above all else. Jesus.

I won't trade that for anything.

6

Speak of Jesus ... Not about Jesus

Notice I didn't say speak "about Jesus." Notice Paul said, "I preach Christ," not "I preach about Christ." So what's the difference? I talk *about* Denver Broncos football. I talk *about* politics and religion, but I speak *of* Jesus. I only speak *of* that which I know. Do we know Him? *Really* know Him? What does it mean to know Jesus? I'd suggest three things:

1. We know Him from what we read about Him. (Although, there's that pesky word *about* again.) I grew up reading a lot of Old Testament and a lot of Paul. For some reason the Gospels felt like the background story to the good stuff. You know, Hebrews and Romans and Galatians and then Revelation when you were megamature.

So I didn't spend a lot of time in Matthew, Mark, Luke, and John. And when I did, it was mostly in John. The synoptic Gospels (the first three) didn't have much theology in them. Just stories of what Jesus was doing. And parables that were odd and confusing. Of course we needed the Gospels to let us know He died and rose again—so we could understand more of the good stuff like justification, atonement, salvation, and redemption. But I never had much time for the Gospels. Seems funny looking back.

Now I tell people that if you want to get to know Jesus, the actual person, then read the four Gospels. Read them until they become part of you. Eat and breathe them. I went through a period in the mid '90s when I read nothing but the Gospels for several years.

Now don't get distracted or misunderstand this point—I think all the books of the Bible are important. All sixty-six of them. They're all helpful. They are all inspired by God. Together they make up His Word. But two things are called "the Word": the Bible and Jesus. All of Scripture points to Him. I remember hearing a story about Charles Spurgeon debriefing his young intern preacher after he delivered the sermon. Dr. Spurgeon told the young man that he did a great job, but that he missed one key element. The young preacher asked what that was. "There was no Christ in your message, son. We preach Christ here at New Park Street Church." The intern was shocked. "But, sir," he replied, "I was preaching from the book of Ezekiel."

Spurgeon responded, "Son, until you can find Christ in Ezekiel you will not share my pulpit again."

Jesus is the Word. Ezekiel is the Word. And then the Word became flesh and lived with us. And now dwells in us. All of the

Bible is helpful, but it is a signpost to the ultimate Word of God—Jesus the Christ. We do not follow the Bible. We don't worship the Bible. We love it because it directs us toward the One who is everything. So while all of the Bible is God's Word, it is not all equal in weight. Is Matthew more important to know than Numbers? Yes. Numbers has its place and it's part of the story and from God's Spirit, but that doesn't mean it carries the same weight of importance Matthew does.

I used to think that in order to share my faith effectively, I had to know and defend the entire Bible. Every single word! Has this ever happened to you? You muster up the courage to finally talk to that person you've wanted to share your faith with … and before you know it … *wham!* They pull out the clobber questions. How can you believe that God created the universe in six days when everybody knows the universe is fourteen billion years old? What about all those people God commanded the Israelites to kill in the Old Testament? Do you actually believe that a whale swallowed Jonah? I feel your pain. It has happened to me, too. I used to get so frustrated until it dawned on me that I don't have to defend or understand everything in the Bible in order to share my faith. Jesus is the point of the Bible. It all points to Him. I don't have to be the Bible's defense attorney. All I have to do is speak of Jesus and He will draw people to Himself.

So reading the Gospels is where I'd start in getting to know Jesus.

2. We know Him by eating Him. Have you ever wondered why Jesus said this in John 6:53–56?

> I tell you the truth, unless you eat the flesh of the
> Son of Man and drink his blood, you have no life

in you. Whoever eats my flesh and drinks my blood
has eternal life, and I will raise him up at the last
day. For my flesh is real food and my blood is real
drink. Whoever eats my flesh and drinks my blood
remains in me, and I in him.

That's crazy talk. The kind of stuff that got Jesus killed. In fact, a
few verses later, we see that many of the disciples no longer followed
Jesus. This teaching was just too weird. But in the gospel of John, the
primary metaphor Jesus uses to describe Himself is that of bread to
eat and water or blood to drink. It's pretty clear Jesus wants us to eat
and drink Him. Not to understand what that means about Him as
a point of theology, but to actually imbibe Him. Inhale Him. So ...
how does that work?

I have no idea.

But here are a couple of my best guesses.

First, I think we need to believe that it's possible to have Him in
us. Really inside of us. Believing that what Jesus asks of us is possible
should always be Point Number One. When He heard the disciples
grumbling (John 6:60–64), He said that He knew some didn't
believe. It seems there is a direct connection between eating Jesus and
faith in Jesus. Maybe they're the same, I don't know. I find conscious
awareness that Jesus is alive in me right now—at this moment—very
helpful. I often (sometimes several times a day) ask myself this question: If Jesus were living my life right now and He were here doing
what I'm doing, would He be pleased or want to do something else?

I think that's a better question than *what would Jesus do?* We can
never be sure what Jesus would do if He were here now. We do know,

however, what Jesus *did.* So I think we should ask this question: Based on what Jesus did (which requires you to know that)—what would He do through me right now, since He lives in me? Or ask it this way: If Jesus had my life to live today, how would He live it?

3. We know Jesus by practicing acting like Him. I'm not really that good at *being* like Him, so I *act* like Him. I'm acting. Pretending. But doing it with the desire to be like Him. That's what I want. But because I'm a knucklehead, I act. Of course, our ultimate dream is to really be Christlike. To have every part of us so in love with God that we find ourselves, almost as an afterthought, like Jesus.

So practice. Practice acting like Jesus. Review the Gospels several times a day. I know them well enough now that I can literally scroll through all eighty-nine chapters and find several examples of how Jesus acted or spoke in a given situation and attempt to do something similar in my current circumstance. You can't imagine how helpful that is if you haven't done it. In order to do so, you have to know the Gospels inside and out and recognize that you have Jesus residing in you by the Holy Spirit's power. Get used to this and it'll change your life. We speak of what we know. Know Jesus and you will speak Jesus.

To close this chapter, I'd like to demonstrate the power of what happens when we strip our "witnessing" of its religiosity and focus simply on the life and teaching of Jesus. A friend of mine named David sent me the story below. May his experience be your experience.

Last summer I was working in northern Canada planting trees. I worked in a camp with about thirty-five other planters. Tree planters have the reputation of being "rough around the edges."

Anyways, as I got to know people within the camp it was clear there was a lot of pain, hurt, and frustration towards Christianity and the church. Yet as I talked about how I was trying to reach out to the poor and marginalized, striving to bring peace into areas of violence and live a life that wasn't consumed with possessions, they were very intrigued and loved carrying on long conversations about these things.

Once again, I discovered that people are so turned off by religion, but yet so attracted to the things that Jesus taught.

So I came up with an idea … I wanted to introduce people to the biblical Jesus—I wanted them to be able to experience Him for who He really was, rather than who people think He was based on our misrepresentation of Him to the world.

Honestly, one of the common questions that comes to my mind when I read the Gospels is, "What the hell?" I kinda laugh thinking about that … I think it's part of my rebellious nature rising up within me, but this truly comes into my conscience when I read. What the hell does this mean? And then, how the hell do we live this out? As I thought about this, I felt like God was saying that this was supposed to be the name of a group. It would not be a "Bible study" because that sounds way too churchy. But the group would be called *What the Hell?* and the purpose would be to read about Jesus and ask two questions: What the hell did Jesus say and how the hell can we live it out?

I proposed the idea to several people and there was overwhelming support for doing something like this. So we did.

I never announced it publicly (to the entire camp at once), but rather let the idea of the group spread more like a rumor or gossip throughout the camp. People were very confused, but interested nonetheless.

At our first meeting we had ten people (it was usually between ten and fifteen), and I gave a quick picture of how I thought we could run the group, but made it clear that I wanted it to be "our" group and not "David's" group. They all liked this and added their input as to how *What the Hell?* would be formatted. I also made it clear that many people view the Bible in different ways—some as the words of God, some as simply good things to live by, etc. I said that no matter where people's beliefs fall, most at least agree there are good suggestions for life within the Bible, and that it would benefit everyone to be aware of what it says. Everyone in the circle shook their heads in agreement. So I did not make it clear that the Bible was inerrant and flawless and gave us ultimate truth, but rather presented it as a book that many people have found helpful as they ask life questions, and that we may be able to learn from the things within it.

We met for probably six or seven times throughout the summer, and mostly stayed within the Sermon on the Mount. Some topics included not judging others, not worrying about the future, loving our enemies, and the stories of the Good Samaritan and the woman caught in adultery. Each night the discussion was lively and everyone enjoyed throwing in their perspectives. I did not see myself as the "leader" but I tried to be a facilitator of sorts, trying to keep the conversation from drifting in different directions.

I would also try to clarify what I thought people were saying so that other people could stay with the discussion. It was difficult at times to bring all the ideas together and reach a conclusion, but all in all, it was a lot of fun! These people that many would consider far from Jesus were seeing Him for the first time, and they were drawn to Him. When they read that Jesus tells us not to judge others they would applaud in agreement; when we talked about caring for the broken and hurting people in our lives, even if it means sacrifice on our parts, they got excited. They could not believe that Jesus stood in front of the stone-throwers to save the life of the woman they rightfully could have stoned.

At the beginning of our meetings they would always be talking about Christians being hypocrites and all that kind of stuff, but we were able to get past that when we admitted that we all fall under the "hypocrite category." But part of me actually likes when they recognize that in general, Christians don't really live up to their title. It is good to realize and admit that being a "Christian" is not always synonymous with trying to follow Jesus. But rather than criticize, we need to get our eyes off of others and just focus on ourselves, our lives, and how we're striving to be the hands and feet of Jesus.

The people attending *What the Hell?* were identifying key characteristics of Jesus' life, and I believe many were drawn to the Jesus we were reading about in the New Testament.

Even though the group had a very "nonreligious" feel, there were still some people who wouldn't come because they thought the Bible was full of crap. But God was working in their hearts as well, and often when I was out planting during the day these people would come up and ask me what we talked about the night before, and I would share the words of Jesus with them. I hope and pray that these individuals were able to catch a glimpse of what Jesus was and still is like.

7

Our Religion Can Beat Up Your Religion!

Remember learning in school about the world's major religious groups? In order of size—biggest to smallest—they are Christianity with about 2.3 billion, Islam with about 1.6 billion, Hinduism almost 1 billion, secular/nonreligious/agnostic/atheist about 800 million, Buddhism about 470 million, Chinese traditional about 460 million, indigenous and tribal groups at 270 million, and Jewish 15 million.[1]

There are a ton of ways we can look at religions—what they mean, who's "in" them and who's not, but for the sake of a starting point let's use the above estimates. If you add up the numbers it does (handily) equal the approximate population of the world. And I think you could make a case for the secular/humanist/agnostic/

atheist group forming a religion as well. These people have beliefs and codes they live by. They are often quite religious about their lack of religion.

Notice that we're winning. Or wait … maybe losing. There are a few ways to see this. Let's examine the possibilities.

Possibility #1: Christianity has 2.3 billion followers. That's the most of anyone. We're winning.

Possibility #2: Christianity has 2.3 billion followers. But the rest of the world is another 4.6 billion—so we're losing and losing badly.

Possibility #3: Christianity has 2.3 billion followers. That includes Catholics and Protestants. Anglicans and Baptists. Pentecostals and Mormons. Jehovah's Witnesses and house churches. So … hmm? A little confusing. How many are "real" Christians? Bible believing? Born again? Jesus following? Who knows? But I do know one source, the *World Christian Encyclopedia,* that claims an answer. It defines a group called "Great Commission Christians" as those who believe the gospel is for everyone and that everyone should know Jesus (others would simply say "evangelicals"). And there are probably fewer than one billion of those.[2] Again, we're losing.

As we've seen, it's hard to know where we stand compared with others. Are there a billion of us? Who is *us?* What about all those folks who call themselves Christians in Serbia or Spain—Orthodox and Catholic—who we might not think have a real friendship with Jesus? Hmm.

So Possibility #4 is to not care about religious distinctions at all.

Who cares if we're winning? Who cares who "we" are in this context? If the standard is actually following the real Jesus—then I'm not even sure *I'm* one of "us." Depends on the day—or the moment. We know the standard can't simply be having good theology. Even demons have that. Or using the label. Or going to church. Or being born in a Christian country and having the name Matthew, Mark, Luke, or John.

What if we just admitted that religious distinctions are helpful for the Sociology 101 class at college but not much beyond that? Religion can be a helpful tool to get you through life, but maybe misses the point. It's okay to go to a building called a church on Sunday at 10:00 a.m. with all your friends and neighbors and family—and do it just because you're a Christian and that's what Christians do on Sunday morning at 10:00 a.m. I'd say that's fine. Even healthy. And it might be okay to feel part of the team—Team Christian. Where we feel we are sometimes winning and sometimes losing. Where we gain our identity and have our schools and colleges and softball teams for men and Beth Moore studies for the ladies. Nothing wrong with it.

Unless it leads you to miss the main point.

The Pharisees were part of Team Judaism. They were pretty good. The whole club thing was going fairly well. They knew and kept the rules. They invited others to join them. They had a clear identity and a clear sense of mission and purpose. They really only missed one thing—Jesus.

Our identity as Team Christian generates many of our challenges when trying to speak of Jesus to our neighbors and coworkers in a way they can hear. If they don't see themselves as part of this winning team, they can feel attacked. We remind them daily in various and sometimes not-so-subtle ways that Team Christian is winning. It's funny, because we don't often think of ourselves as winning. In fact, we usually think we're the underdogs, the ones losing with all the others against us. So why does everyone else feel exactly the opposite?

Let's try to answer both questions—why we think we're losing while, at the same time, they think they are losing. It's weird, but there are reasons why.

First, why do we act and feel like we're on the losing team?

1. Remember there are fewer than one billion of us. That's only one out of every seven people. So six are against us. That's one reason we feel we're behind in the game.

2. We're very aware that even the "others" who say they are part of us really aren't. I grew up Pentecostal/charismatic and I only knew a few things for certain—one was that Baptists weren't really part of us. They thought they were, but they were misguided. Misinformed. Unfortunately deceived. Well meaning, of course. Just wrong. I was shocked to learn, when I finally met one around the age of sixteen, that Baptists thought the same of us. Odd. Most Christians feel attacked even by our own 15 percent of the population, since the "others" don't quite get it either.

3. We are media addicts, and the media generally doesn't represent the will of our 15 percent. If you only watched movies and TV and listened to the radio, you'd be sure that all the world thought abortions were the greatest idea ever. And that everyone thought gay couples should be legally married. And that going to bed with your girlfriend on the first date maybe wasn't the best idea, but after that first one, well you'd be weird if you didn't sleep with her. So we end up feeling like everyone is doing it, and only the few remaining pure

ones on earth are holding out. We feel under attack by our culture. (Whether it's just our media or actually a true reflection of culture is for another discussion.)

So it can seem like Team Non-Christian is winning in a big way. Even though here in the States probably one in every three or four people would put themselves in "our" camp. Whereas worldwide we are one in seven, here the Christian minority seems much larger. At least 38 percent of Americans would identify themselves as born-again Christians.[3] And according to several recent reports, 81 percent of all Americans would still label themselves some kind of Christian.[4] Astonishing.

So Christians in America are not in the minority at all. But we constantly display all the traits of a minority group. Feeling insecure. Under attack. Lacking the power to change things. Fearful. And constantly holding conferences on how we can stem the tide against us. Strange.

Now … why do "they" act like they're on the losing team? Here are a few reasons:

1. We tend to be pretty feisty for a minority group. Loudly vocal. James Dobson. Jerry Falwell. Pat Robertson. Charles Colson. One thing in common—they all have media empires. TV. Radio. Books. Politically active. Very involved in nearly every sector of society. This group knows how to have a fight. Start it or respond to it. Either way. They're up there with Muhammad Ali (maybe not such a good comparison). So it makes the other side feel a bit intimidated.

2. Our structures and institutions are everywhere. Even though they might not be well used, we have to admit that if an alien were

visiting earth and had to make some general observations about life in America, he/she/it would say something like, "There sure is a lot of Christian stuff around here." Churches on every corner. Christian schools for our kids and Christian colleges and seminaries. Sometimes huge and beautiful buildings. Much nicer than anything else in that neighborhood. It just looks like we own the place. *We* might know that those buildings are not full, or if they are, they're not always vibrant—but *they* might not know that.

3. Many of "them" have been on the receiving end of a well-meaning but poorly thought-through evangelistic attempt. If you want to "feel under attack," just listen to someone claiming that unless you agree with him or her, you will spend the rest of eternity in a place hotter than a Phoenix sidewalk in August. Lots of the other 60 percent of Americans and a growing population around the world have experienced similar sorts of evangelism. If you are told you're wrong enough times, it won't take you long to resort to drastic tactics to ignore or compete with those challenging you.

So here we are—at this very strange impasse. Where both sides are actually trying to convince the other (and the onlookers) that *they* are the minority and in the fight of their lives against the evil onslaught of the other. It'd be funny if it weren't so serious.

This book is not about those so-called culture wars or the existence of real evil in the world, but it *is* about speaking of Jesus. And the questions we've raised here are these: Does it affect how we talk about our friendship with and faith in Jesus when we think we're the underdog? And does it affect the hearing of others if they think we're ganging up on them from our bully pulpit? The answer to both is certainly yes.

The remedy: Stop playing the "our religion can beat up your religion" game. It's the wrong game anyway, and as we've seen, no matter how you add up the score, we're losing.

The score isn't six to one.

We aren't even always sure who the other six are. And sometimes we don't know who's on our team. It's hard to play the game when the teams aren't clear.

I hope you're still with me. It's not easy. But it's hugely helpful if you can get this. Ready? Here it is—the thesis of this book: *If you don't feel like you have to evangelize someone away from their team and onto yours, you can speak of Jesus much more freely, and thus, more effectively.*

Not worrying about whether Team Christian is winning or losing is so freeing.

Not feeling like we have the burden to convince the world that they're wrong and we're right allows us to talk about Jesus and how amazing He was and is with total freedom. It's not a contest. There is no score, or at least, we don't know what the score is. There are sheep and there are goats, but we've admitted we sometimes confuse the two. A billy or a ram, a ewe or a nanny, can all look alike from a distance. This doesn't mean they aren't what they are, it just means we may not be as good at knowing the difference as we once thought.

What if we didn't worry/think so much about "those lost people" and simply loved them? To be clear, how about we replace the word *loved* with the words *were nice to?* What if we were just really nice to people? And talked about Jesus constantly? I'm getting ahead of myself, because this is the point of the whole book—be nice and talk about Jesus all the time. It's not rocket science.

I'll never forget the time we were having a team meeting in Beirut. There were ten Americans, a Brit, and one Lebanese woman who had joined us to "church plant" in Lebanon. We had these meetings about twice a week, and they focused on our strategy to get Lebanese Muslims into the kingdom. And then ... into the church. Not a bad agenda (depending on what those terms mean), but it took a lot of time and effort. We prayed, worshipped, did a little study on these methods—mostly from Acts—and then talked. Usually three to four hours each time.

Once, around 10:00 a.m., in the middle of our meeting, there was a knock on our door. We lived on the fourth floor of a five-story building in downtown Beirut and whoever was knocking must have gotten past the locked outer door at the ground floor. It was our friend Hythem. He was a part-time history professor at the American University of Beirut and had stopped by to say hi. Most of us knew him since he had started coming to our semiregular Olive Grove gatherings.

I opened the door, saw it was him, and panicked. He poked his head in and said, "Hey, everyone, what's up?"

We were having a team meeting strategizing about how to reach people just like Hythem: a Lebanese Muslim head of household. Hythem was target number one. But he was interrupting us at a crucial point in our discussion. It was inconvenient and awkward. How could we continue talking about him when he was standing in our doorway?

Honestly, to my great embarrassment, it never occurred to me to invite him in. I made some very awkward, inhospitable comments about why now wasn't a good time and sent him on his way. When

I went to sit back down in my living room with my team, there was an awful silence. But we pulled ourselves together and continued on. Weird, completely weird.

I promised myself that week to never do that again. How silly. How totally upside down that I couldn't think how to engage Hythem in the very thing we were talking about.

Well, God must have heard my prayer because the next week, same time, Hythem showed up. He must have known something. But this time I invited him in. Here's what I said: "Hythem, as you know, most of us have moved to Lebanon because we love God and are trying our best to follow Jesus and help the people of this country. We started the Olive Grove for this purpose. And we need your help. How can we help a people we don't know?

"So … Hythem, what do you think we should do at the Olive Grove?"

That was it. So simple, but it changed everything when we started bringing locals in on the plan.

Relax. Enjoy your friends. Enjoy their company along with the company of Jesus. Point Him out, freely, without fear or intimidation. You're not responsible to sell Him to them. You're simply saying what you've seen. You're not the judge. You're the witness.

We'll go further and further into this way of thinking until you're free to speak of Jesus often and always. And you'll see—people will listen. Not because we're so good, but because He is compelling!

8

Is It Good News?

I'm constantly surprised by how many of my Christian friends seem to revel in the gospel being tough. Hard. Very few will be able to figure it out. Narrow. Camels and needles. Not a broad path. A very narrow path. Offensive. While these words do appear in the Bible, they are both misunderstood and overused.

I remember sitting inside a coffee shop in downtown Colorado Springs with my wife, Chris, and an Italian friend who was close to the kingdom. Suddenly we heard a ruckus outside. It was a man with a big wooden cross and a bullhorn. As we tuned in, we heard him targeting those of us inside the coffee shop. "Perverts, gays, and Catholics," he was yelling, "hell awaits you."

My Italian friend was more than a little uncomfortable. He may not have been a pervert or gay, but he definitely grew up Catholic. I couldn't believe what I was hearing as this man with a cross, a Bible, and a bullhorn made a mockery of our faith. I decided to go outside and confront him. I walked up and said, as kindly as I could, "Brother, I, too, am a Christian, and I'm not sure that what you're doing is the best way to approach things."

With fire in his eyes he quoted (sort of) 1 Corinthians 1:18 and told me the message of the cross was foolishness and that people would be offended by this stumbling block (he used lots of partial quotes from this chapter). All of a sudden, someone ran out of the coffee shop and hauled off and punched the guy right in the mouth. It actually knocked him to the ground. His mouth was bleeding and everyone around was yelling and pushing—I found myself in the middle of a minor riot.

I was torn. This guy was a jerk, for sure. But he didn't deserve to be punched out like a kid on the playground. I leaned over and picked him up, urging him to just go. He did. But as he walked away, he looked at me and said, "Brother, if you're not being persecuted, then what you're preaching isn't real."

Hmm. Again, it almost seems right, but not quite. Or is it? I was so confused. It is true that Jesus promised us persecution. And both Jesus and Peter say we are blessed and should even rejoice when persecuted. So what's the deal? If it's called "good news," and it is, then why would anyone not want to hear it—and even go so far as to persecute the bearers of that news?

I believe there are several issues here:

- Sometimes we are "persecuted" not because of the message but because of our delivery. The guy with the cross was punched because of his delivery style.

- Sometimes we are persecuted because of the perceived politics of the message. This is often the case in the Muslim world. Or with politically liberal Americans—both think our message is tainted with a conservative agenda.

- Sometimes we are persecuted simply because the message of Christ's love and forgiveness just isn't heard, and the person gets angry.

Looking at the life of Jesus, we can surely agree that His delivery was always suited for the time and the person. He was angry in the temple. He was abundantly gracious with the woman caught in adultery. He was slightly less grace-filled with His disciples. Tougher on Peter than on Andrew. Downright mean to the Pharisees. He asked nothing of the healed lepers and the blind and the beggars. Delivered without question the demoniacs and hassled His disciples when they showed little or no faith.

The delivery of Jesus' good news—that the kingdom of God had arrived—changed nearly every time He presented it. But let's assume He always did it right. Were there times the recipients of His message couldn't hear? So many times. The disciples constantly confused His message with their version of politics. They believed Jesus would restore the physical kingdom of Israel. The Pharisees, Sadducees, and Herodians heard Jesus attacking their power base. The Roman leaders heard Jesus wanting to overthrow their empire.

The ones who truly had ears to hear Jesus typically were the hurting, the broken, the desperate. What united the misunderstandings of the disciples, the religious leaders, and the political leaders was an inability to hear the message of the kingdom the way Jesus presented it. They all heard *power*. Either that Jesus was about to give them earthly power or that He wanted to take it away. He was speaking of a whole new way—but they couldn't hear because their ears were clogged with the ways of the world.

And in the end, Jesus died because of this message. Some of the people did understand what He was saying and realized that it was in fact a threat to their way of life. So they crucified Him. Both the Jewish religious elite and the Roman Empire played a role.

Back to the good news being good or not. Remember that, for the most part, the people loved Jesus. They tried to make Him king several times. Even by force. He started preaching the Sermon on the Mount with His immediate disciples listening, and by the end crowds had gathered. Four or five thousand were pretty common numbers for His audiences. Amazing, since there was no advertising in His day. No TV or radio to announce the location of His next campaign. No one knew where He would be holding His next meeting unless they were already following Him, or at least close by.

Who wouldn't like this man? Think about what He did. He healed the sick. Cast out demons from the demonized. Fed the hungry and the poor. Loved sinners. Honored children and women. And was hard on the establishment.

The last part is easy. In America today, it's fashionable to criticize the "Washington DC insiders." It was all too easy to say mean things about President Bush. About 60 percent of Americans didn't like him and let everyone know. Now it's in vogue to do the same with President Obama. The difference is this: Those of us criticizing the establishment aren't following that up by healing the sick, giving sight to the blind, raising the dead, and casting out demons. Just a slight difference.

Luke tells us in Acts that Jesus of Nazareth "went around doing good" (10:38). People tend to like such a person.

Remember the mission statement of Jesus?

> The Spirit of the Lord is on me,
> because he has anointed me
> to preach good news to the poor.
> He has sent me to proclaim freedom for the prisoners
> and recovery of sight for the blind,
> to release the oppressed,
> to proclaim the year of the Lord's favor. (Luke
> 4:18–19)

I find it most interesting that when Jesus quotes this passage from Isaiah 61, He omits the last part. In the original version Isaiah continues with "and the day of vengeance of our God" (Isa. 61:2). Why didn't Jesus say that part?

I believe it was because it didn't fit (at the time anyway) with the *good* part of the good news He wanted to proclaim. For those who were (and are) desperate, Jesus was always good news. He was the one who rescued them. Saved them. But Jesus was a constant threat to the establishment—religious or political.

Bottom line: Most of the time, our presentation of the gospel should come as good news. If it doesn't, let's make sure we're presenting it rightly and doing whatever we can to remove the obstacles so others can hear it.

James, after hearing from Paul and Barnabas the shocking news that Gentiles were turning to God and receiving the Holy Spirit, announced in the first great gathering of church leaders that "we should not make it difficult for the Gentiles who are turning to God" (Acts 15:19). Let's not make it hard to hear and receive this wonderful message of Jesus and His kingdom by our own shortcomings.

Instead of remaining with Team Christian, what if speaking of Jesus leads you into the dens of iniquity? To the places where sinners dwell? To be with outcasts? Muslims? Homosexuals? Liberals? (Or conservatives if you're liberal.) Blacks if you're white or ... I think you get it.

It's fun to think about Jesus being "accused" as a friend of sinners and an imbiber of wine. Seems this was true—He liked to drink wine with sinners. Is that the picture you have of Jesus? A party guy?

Imagine this scene—it's in Luke chapter seven. Jesus has accepted the dinner invitation of a Pharisee, which is in and of itself a surprising thing—showing that Jesus would go anywhere. Jesus is now at the table, resting. Getting ready for dinner. Surely there were others present besides Jesus and this one Pharisee.

In walks a woman of the night. The room gasps. The Pharisee is sure that Jesus will "know" who this woman is and quickly rebuke her and send her on her way. But instead He allows her the unthinkable—her tears wet His feet, she wipes them with her hair, kisses and anoints them with perfume from her alabaster jar.

Wow. A bit sensual, don't you think? Imagine. First of all, how did she know which one was Jesus? She'd obviously seen Him before, maybe out healing the sick or casting out a demon. She seemed to know somehow that she needed Him. That she wasn't worthy of Him. Her actions spoke of pure humility. Brokenness. Asking for healing and forgiveness as she washed the feet of the One who could offer it.

But imagine it from Jesus' side. Or put yourself in His place. Let's say you're a pastor or youth worker at the home of a wealthy religious leader who also happens to be one of your primary donors. And in walks a local prostitute who comes right up to you. What would you do? Would you, in your embarrassment, try to ignore her? Would you quickly explain to the other guests that you do not know her? That you have no idea why she's doing this? Would you push her aside? Stand up and walk away? Turn red? Because Jesus was pure, in heart and actions, He could simply accept her offering. Jesus went on to forgive the woman's sins and then praise her as an example of faith for the shocked Pharisee looking on.

I often make up a similar scenario when I speak. Imagine that I'm standing next to a friend who doesn't know Jesus. And he knows he doesn't know. Maybe he's sort of a rough guy. Tough guy. And he knows he's on the "outside." (It always surprises me how often people categorize themselves as "outsiders.")

I say this: Imagine if Jesus came down right now and was here, physically standing between you and me. Whom do you think He'd prefer? Whom would He want to hang out with? Go have dinner

with? The person always says "you." They think Jesus would want to
hang with me because I'm one of "His guys."

I make a loud beeping noise and lower my hand as if I'm
hitting the buzzer that says "wrong answer." Of course the answer
is the other way around. I explain that Jesus always seemed to
prefer the sinners over the religious guys. Even though I don't
see myself as a "religious guy," I'd probably still be the one on the
receiving end of Jesus' criticism. Maybe I'm the "Pharisee." Or
even a hypocrite in the sense that I don't always do what I preach
to others.

But the outsider would always be on the inside with Jesus as
long as he understood his need. Jesus loved the humility of those
who understood they needed help. That was the issue with the
religious leaders. They didn't know that they needed Jesus. They
thought they had it all wrapped up. They had their theology down.
Their books memorized. Their actions right. They were the conservative religious right of their day. They weren't even the bad guys.
They were the keepers of the law. They were the good guys. The
religious police.

It was just the little detail of missing Jesus. That's all.

So He preferred hanging out with the ones who wanted Him
there. Except on a couple of occasions, the religious leaders felt
threatened by Jesus. The sinners invited Him in. They didn't know
who He was, but they knew He loved and accepted them. That's all
they needed.

If Jesus were walking our streets today, where would He be?
In our churches? Or in a bar? Would He be in Dallas and Tulsa or
Boston and Seattle? Does this mean we should not go to churches,

but bars? Not live in the Bible Belt but the Coffee Belt (Seattle's Best, Starbucks, and Dunkin' Donuts)? Maybe. Or it may just mean that we need to be aware of our tendencies. A tendency to huddle up with our friends on Team Christian. It's easy. Send your kids to a Christian school. Play on a Christian softball team. Hire Christian workers. Go to church on Sundays, Bible study on Wednesdays, and small group on Thursdays. No need to rub shoulders with those pesky wine-bibbing sinners.

Which brings me to my next point …

I realize this may offend some people, but we must ask: When we speak of Jesus, can we do so without speaking of doctrine? The answer is absolutely. Yes and no.

Backing up, what is doctrine? For our purposes, *doctrine* means a set of principles and beliefs taught by the church about God and the Bible. Doctrine is a good thing. We all have doctrines. We all have a theology. It may not be well thought through, but we have one. We may be wrong, but we believe something about almost everything. Paul clearly teaches us to have sound doctrine. Well-studied beliefs about God and His ways so that when we speak of Jesus we know what we're speaking about. Makes sense.

However, where we go terribly off course is *when we lead a conversation with doctrine rather than Jesus Himself.*

Let me illustrate. Several years ago I met with a group of Lebanese doctors. All Muslims. We were in one of their houses and reading through the book of Luke. A new doctor, a friend of the one whose house we were in, showed up in the middle of one such evening. He was surprised to find a group of his friends sitting around reading the Bible with an American guy.

Before he really knew what was going on, he blurted out, pointing at me, "This man is a Christian and believes Jesus was crucified,
how can you be reading the Bible with him?"

After he said this, everyone looked straight at me, waiting for
an answer. Partly because I was dumbfounded, and partly because
I have learned to wait in such situations, I didn't say anything.
After what seemed like an eternity—probably five seconds—the
host said to his friend, "How about you just come on in and sit
down. We were having a good discussion before you came in and
interrupted."

His friend, embarrassed, sat down. We went on. Luke chapter
three. I never said a word. Didn't answer. Didn't defend. And the
man ended up joining our group. Did I agree with him? No. We did
have different doctrines. We did not agree. But fighting over doctrine
at that time would have been a huge error.

Just this week I was chatting with a Jewish businessman who
said, "I do believe in God. But I just can't believe that only the ones
who believe in Jesus Christ are going to heaven." Wow, what a perfect opportunity to talk about his "need" for a Savior. The cross.
Justification by faith in Christ alone. Redemption. And all good stuff
it is. All good news. But do you think this American Jew was ready
to hear that? Don't you think he's heard that *a lot* throughout his life?

Here's what I said. "Hmm. Interesting. How many children do
you have?"

He and his wife, who had just walked in, lit up. They had two.
They talked about them for a while and then the man circled back
around and said, "Hey, wait a minute. Why didn't you answer me

when I said that I don't think you need to believe in Jesus? Aren't you a Christian?"

"Oh," I replied, "I'd just rather talk about your kids than try to convince you of something I believe."

"How refreshing," his wife chimed in. "But you didn't answer my husband. Are you a Christian?"

Again, being careful to answer the real question rather than the stated one, I replied, "I grew up in a Christian home. My religious heritage is Christian, yes. But I am a follower of Jesus."

"What's that?" they both questioned.

I went on to explain what I meant. Why I preferred that label over "Christian." They were amazed. Enthralled. We talked about that point for thirty minutes and at the end of our time—it was late at night—they both said, "We've never heard this before. Can we talk more?"

Now for sure they had both previously heard the "gospel" from well-meaning Christians trying to convert them. They told me so. Why had it not "worked" before? Possibly because the Christians had led with doctrine rather than listening.

Giving someone the "Four Spiritual Laws" or explaining the "Romans Road" or going through "Evangelism Explosion" are not in and of themselves bad things; they just may be ineffective. You know, permissible but not profitable.

9

You're Under Arrest ... for Speaking Christianese!

As the basic communication principle goes, "It's not what I say that matters, but what you hear." One of the most interesting things about Christendom as a culture is that it has developed, over the course of two thousand years, its very own language, including different dialects. It seems that every time a branch group or new denomination develops, it creates its own unique personality, including diction. Specific terms and keywords and catch phrases, all with varying levels of importance. We're human, we have to label everything, you know.

Some of this terminology is helpful; some of it is not. Some of it is correct; some of it is downright unbiblical. Somewhere, in the combination of these terms, words become packed with meanings and implications—useful and otherwise.

As the joke goes, when the old-time, circuit-riding preacher asked the sinner on the side of the road, "Are you washed in the blood?" the confused man looked at himself to check and replied, "I sure hope not."

An example of correct terminology that is not helpful.

I hate to be the one to say it, but maybe we need a "word police." We can mount lights and sirens on hats and pull people over when they use one of the unhelpful or incorrect words. We could even write tickets, impose fines, put people in the pillory, and throw tomatoes and cabbage and pomegranates at them. In love, of course.

We could have a verbal inquisition of sorts, and we could have a secret handshake and decoder rings.

"Halt!" we could shout at people when they're busted. "On your knees, spread your legs. Now repeat after me, 'I will not speak Christianese around other human beings, and if I do so, I will be infested with the fleas of a thousand llamas.'"

Let's think about our words. Like the word *Christian,* which appears only three times in the entire Bible and is so commonly misunderstood today. We've already spoken of the varying responses this word evokes.

I know the word *Christian* is so common and so easy to use that it's almost ludicrous to suggest we get rid of it. Even though I'm pretty sure we'll never stop using it entirely, I never refer to myself as a Christian, although I have to use the word occasionally in reference so people will know what I'm talking about.

It's a completely loaded word, and I think it gets in the way of telling people about Jesus.

"Are you religious?"

"Oh, yes, I'm a Christian."

There's nothing in that exchange that says anything about Jesus.

Also, it doesn't say one thing that is universally consistent. It means different things to everybody.

To most Americans, the phrase *born-again Christian* means "conservative right-wing Republican." I don't know about you, but I don't think that's the idea we want to be spreading when we use those words.

Likewise, in the Middle East, a "Christian" is a descendant of the crusaders, or even worse, a militant who kills Muslims.

To some Europeans, being a "Christian" means some kind of connection to the Roman Catholic Church, which led such noble pursuits as the Spanish Inquisition and selling the forgiveness of sins (indulgences). Or it can mean Protestant, or even the people who burned others at the stake for not being "elect."

In the Far East, and in Africa, the word means roughly the same thing as "Western imperialist." And more often than not, anywhere in the world, *Christian* is a political distinction, separating conservative from liberal, Western from Eastern, one militia from another.

I conclude from this that the word *Christian* is not antibiblical, but it isn't helpful in our contexts. I tell people that I am a "follower of Jesus" instead, because it says it all in three words, and it's definitely more true to the New Testament than the alternative.

Another doozy is the word *church*.

"Now hold on, Medearis, you can't tell us that *church* is unbiblical, 'cause it's not. It's used in the New Testament all the time."

True, however, the word *church* is an English translation of the Greek word *ekklesia,* which is a much more complex noun than plain old *church.* I did some research, looked up stuff in some weird old languages, and sat on my floor with concordances and dictionaries and reference books, and for a few minutes I felt very spiritual and intellectual surrounded by all this theology.

Well, I got over that pretty quick. Most of the references to *ekklesia* define it as an assembly or a congregation of people. There was, however, an old usage of *ekklesia* that meant specific citizens who were "called out" from their peers or from their city. A distinction of separation or of higher status than slaves and noncitizens. Obviously, the early followers of Jesus felt that such a distinction applied to them and that their privileged status of being in God's kingdom constituted some kind of demographic, an assembly or group.

There are over a hundred descriptive correlations to *ekklesia,* and I'm not going to list them all and say that one is the most correct or anything like that, but I do think it's funny that somehow all the language barriers push us into referring to *ekklesia* as some type of building. The word *church* is derived from the older German *kirche,* which refers to a cathedral, another type of building.

The historical *ekklesia* morphed from an "assembly of called-out ones" to an institution; in my opinion, under the auspices of Constantine, emperor of fourth-century Rome. Rather than existing as a growing, dynamic, life-giving organism, the church descended on the people as a structured institution with hierarchies. Interestingly enough, the pantheistic Romans were quick to adopt this new religion. While they had once worshipped many gods with greater and lesser powers and different personalities, they turned to a pantheon of saints with distinct patronages. Mary, Peter, the other apostles, and many since their time have become fixtures in what is known as "church."

I don't believe that is what Jesus intended for His *ekklesia* after He ascended.

We still struggle with the meaning of *church* today. We view church as the building we go to on Wednesday and Sunday, a particular denomination with pastors, elders, laity, and of course a secretary or two.

Back home in Lebanon, I completely discarded the word *church,* and started using another description that I felt was more like the *ekklesia* I had read about.

I invited a young Muslim guy by the name of Ahmed to come to the community center I'd started in Beirut, and he was instantly curious.

"What is it called?" he asked.

"The Olive Grove," I said. "It's a community of faith where people from all kinds of religious backgrounds can come together to find meaning in loving each other and following God."

"So it's a church?" he asked, suspicious.

"Not at all," I said, "and what do you mean by *church?*"

"You know," he said, "like the Catholics. Are you a priest?"

"No," I said, "but, we have some Catholics who come to the Olive Grove. And many Muslims, too. You'll just have to come check it out sometime. We meet on Friday nights, and basically we are trying to learn how to get along with each other and how to get along with God. We've been studying the life of Jesus, and trying to learn from Him."

"Aha!" he said. "So you are a Christian. You believe in Jesus!"

"No, not really." I paused for a second. "Do the Christians you know live and act like Jesus?"

"Well." He looked around. "No. Not really."

"Do you think Jesus was a Christian?"

"Of course." He scratched his head. "Or maybe He was a Muslim."

I don't have a one-word replacement suggestion for *church*. But that's because the concept of *ekklesia* is so much more than any one word can describe. So I propose an experiment. The next time you want to invite someone to participate with you in your spiritual journey, bring him or her to something like an informal small group. Instead of *calling* it a small group or a church group, *describe* what you do. Say that you and your friends are meeting to learn and you're discussing Jesus and His teachings. So on and so forth.

Moving on to another word. Oddly enough, the Bible never calls itself *the Bible*. Actually, the only place you will find that name is on the cover. Perhaps you could argue that *Bible* is what people have always called these sixty-six books, but why throw the old word around and turn people off with it?

Anyway, the Bible *isn't* a book per se. It's a collection of writings written over a period of fourteen hundred years by forty different authors from different countries in different languages. These writings include poems, legal procedures, genealogical records, letters, chronologies, prophecies, and recordings of visions of heaven and earth. Given that there's nothing actually sacred about the word *Bible,* doesn't it seem like such a term may actually be *diminishing* the authority and wisdom of the Word of God?

Just a thought.

Evangelism is another nearly sacred word not found in the Bible. The Greek word *evangel* literally means "good news." It is used 118 times in the New Testament, and 82 of those times it is in the context of a verbal proclamation. *Preach, proclaim,* and *testify* are the three words most commonly conjoined with *evangel.* Although the word *evangelism* isn't in the Bible, there is a biblical precedent for it as a concept.

But there is a better phrase, one I think is more biblical: the commandment to *make disciples.* True, it only appears once, in Matthew 28:19, but it is a significant command, and it was Jesus' final one. Ironically, this verse is used mostly as a call ... to evangelism. Ha!

This word is harmful, at least in my opinion, simply because it endorses a flawed concept.

Evangelism, as a method, is dangerous because it's something we "do" to other people. Nobody likes to be "done." Remember the last time the guys in white shirts rode their bikes up to you and tried to tell you that you needed to get saved or whatever? Not fun. It actually feels a little violating to have somebody "do it" to you. Icky.

Also, because evangelism is an *-ism,* it encourages people to think of it as a philosophy or methodology as opposed to a lifestyle. Think of all the recent books that have tried to dispel that myth by encouraging "lifestyle evangelism" or "friendship evangelism." These were noble attempts, but they never really got off the ground because the language barrier was still at the core of the problem.

Evangelism tends to be event oriented and program driven. We think of a Billy Graham crusade, or try to get people "pushed through" a series of four or five concepts and a prayer that supposedly guarantees salvation, which is, by the way, a totally unbiblical notion.

A friend and I were talking about this just the other day. "Why are so many Christians so weak in their faith and their walk?" he asked me.

"Well," I said, "I think part of the reason is that we tend to promote the evangelism method of spreading Christianity rather than the discipleship model of Jesus. We get people 'in' and then try to go out and get others. After a while, everybody's 'in' and nobody has any idea how to mature in their faith."

Evangelism leads people to believe that it is a job done solely by evangelists. Therefore, very little actual evangelism, or whatever we're going to call it, is ever done.

Making disciples, as opposed to evangelism, is a journey of relationship that encompasses support, trial and error, and difficulty. It isn't based on the explanations and doctrines of a religious system.

Evangelism leaves hurt people hurt, sinful people sinful, and religious people religious. Discipleship is a journey that requires change, whereas evangelism is just information. Information, in case you didn't know, is pretty poor at effecting change by itself.

Discipleship involves time commitment. If you love someone, you will spend time with him or her, talking about the things you love. Evangelism, since it is event oriented, tends to appear only at annual conferences and the last thirty seconds of a sermon when a pastor makes a quick altar call.

Another word that tends to front a faulty concept is *missionary.* I'm not going to spend a lot of time on this one, first of all, because it doesn't appear in the Bible. Although, biblically, it is halfway right in terms of its ideal. The closest biblical word is *apostle,* which means delegate or messenger. Somebody sent.

The word *missionary* has the same problem *evangelism* does. It doesn't mean what we'd like it to mean.

Hundreds of times people have asked whether or not I am a missionary. At first I pretended to be offended at the label, but over time, as I gathered experience, I discovered I didn't have to pretend as much as the careless stereotype actually did offend me.

I was teaching a class at the American University of Beirut one day, and after the class, a young man came up to me and asked bluntly if I was a missionary.

"Are you kidding?" I asked. "What makes you think I'm a missionary?"

"You were talking about Jesus earlier," he said, "and I thought that you were a Christian missionary."

I held a hand to my forehead, appalled. "Are you saying," I asked, "that I'm one of those people who wants to spread capitalism and democracy and political idealism and Westernism and import a new religion?"

He looked at me, suspicious. "Well, that is what missionaries do, isn't it?"

"Yes," I said, "typically. Now tell me, do I look like a person who would *ever* be interested in changing your culture, obliterating your heritage, and making religious converts? Why would I do that? There's nothing sensible or right about that, is there?"

"Of course not." He held up his hands. "Look, I didn't mean to offend you, but I just had to ask."

"Why?"

"Because …" He trailed off, unsure of what to say.

"Because you don't trust missionaries," I stated.

He nodded. "Honestly, yes. I thought maybe you had an agenda, and I wanted to find out. Sorry if I offended you."

"Don't worry about it," I said. "Look, if you *are* interested in anything, just let me know, but don't worry that I'm here to subvert your culture or anything, because I'm not. My interest in Jesus has nothing to do with religion, okay?"

"All right, Mr. Medearis. I'll see you later."

One of the problems with being a *missionary* is that it's a term you avoid even if you are one, although everyone else around you will refer to you as a missionary, making it uncomfortable and even deceitful at times. If the people you are trying to reach have you pegged as a missionary, you're going to have to work twice as hard to get to them.

Back in the country sending the missionaries, more problems stem from this unhelpful word.

Missionary can mean somebody who couldn't "cut it" in his or her native culture, who seeks the travel and missionary lifestyle as a refuge as opposed to a calling.

Alternatively, there is something about the whole missionary concept that can swing to the other extreme: the distinction of being heroic and overly exalted.

One of the strangest dynamics around missions is what I call the "surrogate suffering syndrome"—the reliance of others on the so-called missionary to produce fruit or to suffer from a difficult lifestyle, providing a productive feeling to the "folks back home" giving prayer or financial support.

Any tree growing like this would be lopsided and malnourished, with a strong leeward side and a skeletal windward side. With such an incongruous and unhealthy growth pattern, the tree would grow only on the side away from the wind and the resistance, with only a few brave buds popping out where existence is more challenging.

As I speak around the globe at different venues, people often approach me after a session with the same question.

"Carl, you just spent the last three hours cutting and breaking and tearing up all the stuff that we know. Now you say we're not *Christians,* you say we don't *convert* people, we're not *missionaries,* we don't go to *church,* and we don't *evangelize.*"

"So what's your question?"

"Well, uh ... I guess it is: Who are we and what *do* we do?"

I have never come up with anything better than to say, "We are people trying to follow Jesus." As simple (and complex) as that.

10

Jesus the Folk Hero

Jesus is a baffling figure. One thing that baffles me most is what Jesus did and *didn't* say to people He touched. He often did *not* tell them to repent. He just healed them. Sometimes He said not to tell anyone. (They did anyway.) Before He told the woman caught in adultery to "sin no more," He asked her where her accusers were and said, "Neither do I condemn you"(John 8:11). He gave the blind sight, the lepers clean skin. He healed women and the demonized and spoke to Samaritans—often not asking anything from them.

Think about all the people whom Jesus interacted with during His life and ministry:

The religious leaders.

His disciples.

The crowds that followed Him around.

Women and children.

Lepers, prostitutes, the demonized, and the Samaritans.

Ask yourself these two questions—whom was Jesus hardest on? Whom was Jesus easiest on? It seems that He was hardest on the ones who were close to Him and easiest on those furthest away. If that's true—why?

Perhaps … those who think they're "in" or that they know the way or have the truth need a bit of shaking. Legalism is the enemy of Jesus. It's not that we cannot know truth—not at all. As much as Jesus has us, we have truth. So we *can* know truth. We can know a lot of things. But as soon as our attitudes shift from a humble "knowing" of Jesus to a know-it-all type of arrogance, we're toast. We will be on the rebuking end of Jesus' words.

Up to this point, we have been stripping things away from the truth, like an archaeologist brushing sediment away from an artifact. We've been excavating the idea that salvation—the gospel, the central message, the spiritual reality behind religion—hinges on one person, the person of Jesus, and not on the lists and manifestos we have built over the centuries.

And sometimes those we think are "furthest away" have a greater appreciation for Jesus than those of us "nearest" to Him.

I was staying with friends at a hotel in Basra, Iraq, in the spring of 2003. While there, we managed to attract the curiosity of the hotel staff. They were curious about this team of international people staying at their hotel. Since a war was well under way, they were all the more intrigued because we weren't wearing camouflage and toting M4 carbines. During the day, out in the streets, we had given out all of our texts—Arabic translations of the gospel of Luke. We were checking in for another day and as we stood in the lobby near the front desk, the hospitality manager leaned across the counter and looked at me.

"Why have you come here?" he asked in English. "Are you with the American army?"

"No," I said, "we followed Jesus to Basra, so we are trying to find out what He is doing here."

He took in his breath with a hiss. "Isa?" he asked, using the Muslims' name for Jesus. "Isa is in Basra?"

"We think so," my friend Samir said, "and He wants us to help out in any way we can."

The manager made something like a gasping sound and snatched the phone off the cradle. He rattled off a quick sentence in Arabic, hung up, and came around in front of the desk. "If you please," he said, "stay right here. I know you must be very busy, but I had to call my brother. He loves to hear about Isa."

Samir and I looked at each other. Isa was in Basra after all.

Within a few seconds, three other men joined us, all in their twenties and thirties, wearing the dark blue uniform suit of the hotel staff. For a moment I wondered if they were going to ask us to leave. Then, one of the men, with black hair and a thickening moustache, rushed forward and shook my hand. He moved on down the line, shaking hands vigorously, his eyes lit up like candles.

"You know about Isa?" he asked, returning to me.

"Yes," I said, in Arabic. "We followed Him here."

"Oh my." His hands shot to his face. "Let me tell you something," he went on. "When I was a young boy, a man came through our city, and he was telling stories about Isa to the people."

The rest of the group and the hotel staff moved closer, listening intently.

"When this man left, he gave my father a cassette tape with recordings of the stories of Isa, the miracles and teachings of Isa, the people He talked to, and how He lived."

"Wow," I said.

"Every night, for ten years, my father would play the tape for me and my brothers and sisters. He played it until the tape did not work anymore." He stopped for a second, caught his breath. "I love these stories of Isa, and I miss them."

"Well," I said, "we—"

He cut me off, excited. "I have heard, from my father and the old men of the city, they say that there are books, sacred books, ancient books that tell the stories of Isa, as they happened, by the friends of Isa. Is this true?"

"Yes," I said, "and as a matter of fact, we have been giving them out all day."

He almost fainted. I could see his face color, then pale, then color again. He was vibrating with excitement. "Oh please," he said as he gripped my hand, "you must find one for me, you must give me one. I have to have one."

"All right," I said, and turned toward the elevator, "I'll see if I've got one left."

As I rode the elevator up to my room, I realized I was nearly shaking from the same excitement.

I almost never see someone who cares about the stories of Jesus like this man did. It's rare. Back in the States, sermons and teachings often revolve around doctrine, theology, and how to live a more fulfilling life. We seem to have forgotten the power and the humility and the sheer genius of Jesus, His vibrancy and His compassion. To the man in the hotel, Jesus was the ultimate folk hero, a person of mystery and influence, and he was ecstatic about finding the stories of Jesus again. He was thirsty.

When I speak in the States, so often the dialogue deteriorates to discussions about church planting, having a purposeful life, or the doctrinal differences between denominations. Sometimes it even goes so low as tithing and worship problems, or water immersion versus other methods of baptism. Almost never does anyone want to talk about Jesus, His stories, teachings, miracles, and compassion for sinners. Jesus isn't a folk hero in America; He's a lost relic, an artifact from another age.

The elevator dinged and startled me out of my reverie. I needed to find this man a gospel, or he was going to pull his hair out. Or maybe the hotel rates would rise, who knows. Anyway, he needed the stories of Jesus like he needed water and air, and I wanted him to have one almost as bad as he needed one.

I tore my room apart. I ripped open my suitcases and threw my clothes all over the room. A shirt hung from the bathroom doorknob, a pair of socks stuck in the lamp. Finally, after scrabbling around in my luggage like a miner digging for ore, I found one. A gospel of Luke. In Arabic, the title was something like "the gospel of Luke, a follower of Jesus." I snatched it, raced out of the room, and rushed for the lobby.

I will never forget his face when I handed it to him. With tears on his cheeks he held it reverently, lifted it to his forehead, and closed his eyes. He lowered it to his lips, gave it a kiss, and then slowly opened it to look at the print. He lovingly ran his fingers over the pages, and then bolted for the lobby desk. He picked up the phone, dialed rapidly, and spoke even faster. When he hung up, he looked at me and said, "I had to call my father; he will know if these are the same stories of Isa as I heard before."

We waited for a few minutes, and after some time an aging Iraqi man showed up—gray beard and all. He looked at us a little suspiciously at first and made his way over to his son, who was literally popping up and down with excitement.

"Papa," he said, "these men have come here because they are followers of Isa. I told them about the stories of Isa on the tape, and asked them if they had heard of the writings of the stories, and they gave me one of them."

The old man came closer, picked up the gospel, and lifted it to his face. He read the title, thumbed through the pages, pausing to read here and there, and then he stopped, lifted the book to his lips and kissed it, tears in the corners of his eyes. "Yes," he said, "this is it. These are the stories of Isa." He wrung our hands, hugging us to his body, so grateful that he shook.

It's that way in many places in the Middle East. I have been flooded, mobbed, and nearly crowded into the trunk of my car just for handing out these stories of Jesus to people who yearn for Him, as they should.

Now that's not to say that the rest of the Bible is invalid or unimportant, but simply suggests that Arabs have a soft spot for

Jesus—like so many others have—and in some ways, more than we do here in the West.

This is a rebuke, in case you didn't notice. But please, please don't close this book unless you're opening the stories of Jesus instead. I'm not telling you any of this so that I can feel superior or make royalties or just make you feel bad. I'm telling you this because I know how powerful and dynamic Jesus becomes when unleashed to live His life at the center of ours.

We have forgotten how important it is that Jesus came as a human and lived a personal human life. While the cross is the favorite symbol of Jesus in the Western arena, to the Eastern mind, Jesus is like Robin Hood or Ivanhoe or Christopher Columbus. He is the stuff of legend. He is the personification of a holy prophet, and yet a man of the people. He is a hero.

What's interesting is that Muslims don't believe in the martyrdom of Jesus—His sacrifice for our sins—which is, ironically, the only thing the Western world seems to remember about Him. This is like being a fan of Dr. King or Mahatma Ghandi without actually knowing what either stood for. Idolizing somebody only for his death is a cheap fake compared to trying to live up to his life and words.

Dallas Willard, author of *The Divine Conspiracy*, points out that, for the most part, the rank and file of Christendom has no idea how to actually live in the paradigm of Jesus. He's not pointing the finger to make a buck or to make everybody feel bad. He's trying to reassert the importance of the humanity and life of Jesus Christ.

What I appreciate about Willard's approach is that he begins by pointing to Jesus, the person. The man, Jesus of Nazareth. Likewise,

Philip Yancey, an editor for *Christianity Today*, writes about the life and humanity of Jesus in his book *The Jesus I Never Knew*. Both authors compare Jesus' life and teaching with what comes from some pulpits in the modern church.

Their diagnosis? Living a life like Jesus must begin with being a student of Jesus. This is the seed of discipleship.

Because Jesus approached us, in our territory, in our skin, clothed in humanity, we must respect Him that way. We must realize that His approach as a man was not out of desperation; it was not plan B or just an off-the-cuff idea He and His Father thought of at the last minute. It was the great plan all along. And it was done according to prophecy, the way God had intended from the beginning. We must begin by respecting Jesus, the man.

The Western church has made the mistake of deifying Jesus too quickly. It's not that He isn't God, or that He isn't worth deifying, it's that He waited for years before He revealed Himself to the people in that way. He deliberately established Himself by proclaiming His message, being baptized by His cousin John, and being tempted according to His flesh—according to the weaknesses of His humanity. Throughout His entire ministry, He was clothed in supernatural power only three times. First, on the mountain with Moses and Elijah; second, during the period of His resurrection; and then finally, at His ascension to heaven. The rest of His ministry was in the frailty of humanity.

And Jesus was a prime specimen of humanity. Perhaps not in the looks department, and certainly not in the social department. Judicially, He was in serious trouble. But He was brilliant. He was a first-rate teacher with a mastery of communication, particularly what we know today as the Socratic method.

He was a natural leader, and His favor with people was so broad that His disciples ranged from ascetic Essenes to a government-sanctioned tax-collector to a Zealot—the Jewish revolutionary of the time. This is like having a ministry team comprised of a monk, a freedom fighter, and an IRS official. His disciples also included a handful of lower-class fishermen and other blue-collar workers.

Jesus appealed in one way or another to all of them. He was never deceitful, He never pandered to them, and He didn't play favorites. So how did He manage to assemble a team of such diverse individuals?

Because He was genuine. He was masterful. He had keen insight and cared deeply for people. He was, in terms of His humanity, an attractive personality, the upper crust of natural intelligence, and a grassroots-recognized leader. He was the man other men look to for sincere answers, for hope.

One of my best friends is an author by the name of Ted. Ted mostly writes fiction, although he has recently released a nonfiction book titled *The Slumber of Christianity*. I've known Ted for many years, and I could actually see this book coming for a long time. Ted believes, to the core of his heart, that all people thirst for the pleasure of hope. He believes that above all, Jesus was the embodiment of hope, the personification of a pleasure, which, as Ted would say, exists in a kingdom that hides behind the skin of this world.

Ted is addicted to this hope. He respects Jesus because Jesus did something humanly impossible while clothed in human skin. He offered real, lasting hope. Ted's contention is that Jesus was masterful because He brokered the hope of heaven while He lived on earth. As it happens, I agree, although I'm not nearly as animated about it as

Ted is. Once, we were sitting in his office going over some writing ideas. He was in the middle of writing a novel and also editing *The Slumber of Christianity* at the same time.

"Look," he said, thumbing through some pages, "it's funny writing nonfiction." He set the manuscript down on his desk, got up, and started pacing. Ted does this when he gets going. He paces, ruffles his hair, and then gets into the role of whatever character he happens to be writing about. "The funny thing about it is that for once, my readers are going to take me seriously. They're going to listen to what I have to say about something. My opinion matters. Supposedly." He did the hair ruffle thing again. "And you know what?"

"What?" I asked.

"I really don't think modern Christianity needs anything … except Jesus."

"Yeah," I said, "and boy do they need a lot of Him."

I'm not one of those people who have epiphanies. I don't sit underneath trees on the mountaintops and contemplate the meaning of life. I don't burn incense in my office or meditate three hours a day. But I have spent most of the last two decades talking about Jesus, and you can't do something like that for such a long time without some of it actually hitting home. When I first started my career as a missionary, I was full of ideas. I had a message so big it took a moving company to transport it. During twenty years of sharing my faith, I learned that there's really only one thing that's important, and that is Jesus Himself.

The key to following Jesus is by beginning to see Him as another person. The way He came to us. If we are too quick to deify Him, we move Him into the realm of mysticism, to the nebulous ethereal place where things are so strange and otherworldly that they are important only in some spiritual context.

The really neat thing about accepting Jesus as a person is that it makes our experience with Him real. Living with a real person forces us to live honestly. Like in a friendship. Instead of living by some moral code, or conjuring up some spiritual state of mind, all we have to do is make our life about a relationship with a person. God has shortened the distance between us by coming here, and He has made the kingdom of heaven available in friendship form.

By accepting God as a man, we are accepting the invitation of heaven as it is offered.

It actually takes more trust in God to step back from our understanding of Him so that He may explain Himself. We have, for so many years in the West, used every logical tool in our box to define and explain God. To make Him palatable to our sense of reason. We have apologetics and creation science; we have arguments and doctrines, but all of these things exist to explain God to us. We have religion as a substitute, God by proxy.

Jesus changes all of this. Jesus is our God. Jesus can be our folk hero. He can be our leader, and our friend.

We must allow Him to be a man.

11

Confused about Jesus ... and That's Okay!

A few years ago a friend of mine, whom I'll call Ali, came to me with a problem. He was a Muslim and a part of one of my regular groups. We were studying the methods of various leaders, and eventually, my Muslim friends decided we should examine the prophet Jesus. In case you didn't know, Jesus is a very important person to Muslims. He is noted as the only *sinless* prophet of Islam and mentioned over eighty times in the Qur'an, the holy book of Islam. While Christians are the object of "fear and trembling" to many Muslims, Jesus is not. But within Islam, He is not equivalent to God, nor was He crucified.

Our group had been meeting and discussing Jesus' principles, and this young man began to read the "stories of Jesus," or as we call them, the Gospels. He was in awe of Jesus' authority and wisdom, but stumbled upon the teaching found in Matthew 5:44.

"Carl," he said, "Jesus has said to do something that is impossible." He was obviously perplexed.

"Like what?" I asked.

"He says that we should love our enemies, that we should pray for people who persecute us."

I paused. I wasn't sure what he was getting at. "Well, Ali," I said after a minute, "there's a lot of things that Jesus said to do that are difficult to do, and you know that I don't do most of them, and I am a follower of Jesus."

"That's not the point, Carl," he said. "The problem is that Jesus either knew this was impossible, and wasn't disturbed by it, or worse …" He trailed off. "Or He didn't know that it was impossible, which means that He was *wrong*."

Let me hit the pause button on this story for a moment. What was I to do? I had a Muslim friend interested in Jesus, and moreover, he was *seriously studying the teachings of Jesus, with the idea of obeying them*. Who gave him *that* idea?

"Maybe," I said, "Jesus said that so that we would stop and think exactly what we're thinking right now."

"You mean He wants me to worry?" Ali asked.

I didn't know what to say after that, so I shrugged.

While I didn't exactly brighten his day, I did put a bug in his ear, so to speak. Within weeks, he had not only read the Gospels, he had started buying every commentary he could find, just to get every possible perspective he could on the mysterious nature and teachings of Jesus.

I don't know where Ali is in his search for answers. I don't know if he's "in the circle" or "out of the circle." And frankly, that's not important. What's important is his instinctive reaction to Jesus. He didn't just drop to his knees and say, "Okay then, count me in."

He fights, like a fish on a hook.

Struggle. What if struggling with Jesus is a part of Jesus' plan?

"Wait," you might be saying, "is this guy a Christian or not?"

If that's what you're thinking, then you're still missing the point, and you really need to hear this: It doesn't matter if Ali fits our definitions. What does matter is that he's trying to follow Jesus.

His struggle with Jesus' teaching is more profound than any five-point salvation message anyone could deliver. So the answer is, *I don't know*. But I do know this: He may be a Muslim, but he's right where Jesus wants him.

I believe, very sincerely, that we should all be a lot more confused. Seriously. I mean, why do we make such a big deal about having everything figured out? Why do we feel that we're below par when we don't?

Maybe we don't actually have anything figured out, and we're all just faking it.

One of my friends and I were talking about this the other day. He said, "Carl, how come everybody is always ripping on the disciples?"

I thought about it for a second. "You know, probably because they made so many mistakes."

"Yeah, so?" he asked. "See, that's the thing, right there. Everybody assumes that we're somehow superior to Peter and John and the others. We think we're smarter, we think ..."

I picked up where he left off. "We think that we wouldn't be as bewildered by Jesus if we were in their shoes."

"Exactly," he said. "Take Peter, for example. Everybody always makes fun of Peter for sinking while trying to walk on the water. We make an example out of him, and we use him to makes points for sermons."

"Yeah, I know," I said, "I heard it a couple of weeks ago. The pastor said, 'Peter sank because he took his eyes off Jesus.'"

"I was just gonna say that," he said, "but do we actually know that's why Peter sank? Anyway, the point is, we spend so much time laughing at Peter for sinking, when in reality, every single one of us would probably have stayed in the boat, right?"

"Absolutely. Matter of fact, I would have tied myself to the mast."

"I'd be right next to you, wetting my pants."

I laughed. "Probably a tunic."

He looked at me. "How do you wet a tunic?"

"I don't know, but I'm thinking you could probably figure out how."

As I was driving home afterward, I realized that our conversation was deeper than I'd thought. Something mysterious was swimming around in my head, something I couldn't figure out about Jesus. Typical.

He was so confusing to the disciples. Actually, He was confusing to everybody. His teachings were so upside down, so unheard of, that He flat out baffled everybody who listened to Him.

After a few days of thinking about it, I realized my friend was making a point I'd been trying to pound home for years. Somehow, we think that because we're "Christians" and because we go to church and because we have the Bible and because we've heard stories and sermons and went to school—we think that makes us smart, sharp, and oh-so-modern people. We can't be fooled. We won't be baffled. We would do so much better than the disciples. We would have the plan figured out with a snap of the fingers. Easy as pie, right?

But I think that's a load of junk. And I think it's arrogant, too. I think we forget that Jesus astounded the elders, teachers, and priests in the temple when He hadn't even hit puberty yet. We forget that Jesus confounded the wise, humbled the intellectuals, and left the educated rocking on their heels with something to think about.

Jesus could always outwit and outmaneuver any egghead or philosopher, and the fact that He was born two thousand years ago does not mean He was simpler than us just because the public education system of the time was, er ... lacking, shall we say.

Maybe we discredit His insight and wisdom because He spoke to people who didn't know what a Cartesian plane was. Because they'd never read Plato's *Republic,* because they'd never taken a course in algebra or studied apologetics.

If Jesus were to drop into my little writing studio to talk, He would completely outwit me. He proved Himself to the most capable minds in Jerusalem—why do I assume that I'm more qualified because I know some theology?

Knowing about all the "Christian" stuff and going to yearly conferences does not mean that we're in line with Jesus.

If I were to experience a similar discipleship to the person of Jesus, I would be every bit as silly and moronic and confused

and unreasonable as Peter and the others. Jesus would baffle me
completely.

Come to think of it, He does.

One minute we're not supposed to be angry, not supposed to
even think about lusting; we're supposed to love our enemies, pray
for terrorists, and yet we're not supposed to practice righteousness
in front of people—so they won't notice? I'm a bit confused. If you
loved your enemies, didn't lust, and didn't get angry with people, you
would stick out like a sore thumb.

He even said that our prayer lives should be a secret between
us and God. The truest prayer is the one said earnestly when we are
alone with God. When we pray overtly in front of others, it is easy to
derail the genuine communion of our hearts before God and replace
it with something that sounds nice, something that others want to
hear or think impressive.

Jesus commanded forgiveness toward others as a key component of being forgiven ourselves. In fact, He said, "If you do
not forgive men their sins, your Father will not forgive your sins"
(Matt. 6:15).

One step further. What about the so-called War on Terror? I can
think of no greater persecution in our time than the horrific slaugh-
ter of people in acts of terrorism. If we are hated, then terrorists are
the haters. And Jesus commands us to love them.

We can't simply pull in our church boundaries, tell the rest of
the world to drop dead, and then bomb the sand out of the Middle
East. At least not if we are trying to follow Jesus. The conservative
movement here in the West often tries to embrace the moral code of
Christianity without the self-sacrificial teachings of Jesus.

My friend Phil hates it when I start talking about this love-your-enemies stuff. He's a conservative, and he used to be in the military, so he liked the idea of bombing anything. If you saw him, you'd understand. He once said to me that we should invade Canada to stop the spread of the metric system. I laughed for a second, and then noticed he was a bit serious.

"Phil," I said, "you have a Jesus fish tattooed on your back, and you want to invade Canada to stop the spread of the metric system?"

He grinned. "Well," he said, "ya gotta have priorities, mate."

I was driving up Academy Boulevard in Colorado Springs the other day, which is not fun. It was four thirty in the afternoon and the traffic was starting to get nasty, which meant that we were moving approximately one block every two weeks or so. I had a beard by the time I got home. Anyway, since I had time, I edged up behind a car that was covered in bumper stickers. You know how some cars have really funny bumper stickers, and you can't help but read them? This wasn't one of those cars. At least not on purpose. Anyway they had a campaign bumper sticker exactly above a Christian bumper sticker, and I could tell that whoever had put the stickers on hadn't really thought through how it would read. Both stickers together read exactly like this:

**BUSH
& CHENEY
Jesus is the Answer!**

I lost it. I laughed so hard that the soda I was drinking came out of my nose and burned my nostrils. I was thinking that it would be tough to sell the good news of Jesus to an enemy of the United States with this unlikely trinity of Bush, Cheney, and Jesus.

Don't get me wrong, I'm not Bush bashing here, and I'm not going to get political. That's not my intention. I'm trying to make the point that we in the West have often adopted what I call the "fortress mentality," which says it's okay to oppose other people out of self-preservation. If Jesus had done that, we'd be in trouble.

For some unknown reason, Christians are known almost universally as the people who are "against things." Here in Colorado Springs, where I live now, our city is divided politically and socially, and battle lines have formed on both sides of almost every issue imaginable. My friend Phillip describes it as "Briargate vs. Downtown: a home game where all the players get injured and nobody wins."

The Briargate area of town is, for the most part, the bastion of conservative evangelical Christianity, home turf for some pretty big ministries and nonprofit organizations. The downtown area, on the other hand, is a haven for the gay and lesbian crowd, for the tattooed, the pierced, the outcasts, and the revolutionaries. It's the home turf for a lot of the liberals.

As a result, there's always a rally or a picket line somewhere in town. Feelings are pretty heated about current issues as it is, and sometimes the name-calling and the mudslinging reach newsworthy status.

For many conservative Christians, the arguments are about social policy, political activism, and countering the so-called liberal agenda of the homosexuals, the abortion-rights people, and sometimes just about anybody else who believes differently.

For liberals, there are protests and rallies to undermine or outshout the "Christian conservatives."

I'm from Beirut, which, as everybody knows, is where conflict was invented. So when I got back to Colorado Springs, my first inclination was to find conflict and have a cup of coffee in the middle of it. Conflict is universal in one sense—people straining to "get them before they get us."

Jesus lived during a time of serious oppression and political/military conflict. There were wars, outbreaks, public executions, revolutionary groups, and counterrevolutionary groups.

One day I took a notebook and went downtown to Poor Richard's, which is a restaurant, bar, bookstore, and toy store all rolled into one. The owner, Richard Skorman, is a very dear friend of mine. He's on the city council and, among other things, is the local champion and go-to guy for gay-rights issues. Not a conservative Christian. There are about eighty-five coffee shops I could go to just in my own neighborhood, but for some reason, I like it better down at Poor Richard's, even though it's a half hour drive from my house.

Anyhow, as I was saying, I went, took a notebook, and started polling every person I could get my hands on. I wanted to test out some word associations. I worked for a couple of hours, and I got some surprising results. The most striking responses I got were the replies to questions like "What do Christians do?"

What do Christians do?

Eighty-five percent of the people I polled said the same thing, each in different words: "Christians are against things. They fight us and judge us and they hate us."

That should set us all back on our heels.

Often Christianity becomes affected by bottom-line theology, and the proof is in our political allegiances, our social outcries, and, above all, our reputation as the people who are "against things."

Guess what Jesus was never accused of? Of being against things. He wasn't defined by His hatred of things. Imagine if He were.

"Here comes Jesus, the sin-hater."

"Jesus, Son of David, opposer of liberals, have mercy on me, a sinful man!"

Or, Jesus asks the disciples ...

"Who do the people say that I am?"

"Easy, Jesus." Peter raises his hand. "You're against the Romans, the Samaritans, the barbarians, and the French!"

Defining somebody by their opposition would be like labeling a football team by their rivalries. "Featuring tonight, on Monday Night Football, the team that trumped the Titans, smashed the Steelers, foiled the Falcons, junked the Jets, and grounded the Giants!"

The definitions my liberal/gay friends gave Christians would read like a rap sheet on Al Capone.

So where did they get the idea that we are the people who are "against things"?

They didn't get it from Jesus, that's for sure.

Just to check, I asked them what "Jesus" meant to them. Only three of them associated Jesus with Christianity.

"Medearis, get a grip," you might be saying. "You can't put this one past us. If you poll liberals and gays you're going to get a loaded answer!"

Maybe so. It's okay, I'm not running God's reelection campaign, so I don't have to prove anything to keep my job. But I wanted to see if the non-Christians were interested in Jesus at all.

Answer? A resounding yes. Almost all of them gave me the unqualified answer that they would follow Jesus as long as He didn't have anything to do with Christianity. Interesting, no? What makes Jesus so attractive and Christianity so *unattractive?*

I believe it's the way of Jesus.

Jesus' way was a way of humility, a lifestyle of service without self-exaltation. It was the way of foot washing, the way of meekness, the way of preferring others, of living for the glorification of something bigger.

Jesus' way was the way of big dreams. When He initially sent out the twelve disciples, He gave them a task that was much, much bigger than anything they could accomplish on their own. Jesus' way required big faith. Jesus knew that giving His friends an unimaginably huge task would require their reliance on Him and inspire their passions, fanning them into a bonfire that would last long after He was gone.

Jesus' way was not religious. Jesus knew how to work within the religious boundaries of the time, without becoming religious Himself. His teaching centered on bringing the prophecies of the Torah to bear upon Himself. His parables and stories were illustrations of the kingdom of heaven.

Jesus' ease within the religious system came from His confidence. He knew who He was. This gave Him great power and freedom, an ability to be comfortable in any part of the world, and yet not be of it. Jesus didn't start a new religion called Christianity. He lived in relationship, and He extended relationship. This was Jesus' way.

Jesus' way was patient and kind. A cursory glance at the Gospels tells us it took the twelve disciples three years with Jesus and Pentecost before they understood, before they really knew what was going on. And yet, during His three years of ministry, we see Jesus' impatience with the disciples only once or twice, and not because of a lack of progress—because of a lack of faith. Jesus lived as an example of extraordinary patience. Throughout the Gospels, we see the disciples repeatedly asking dumb questions, making mistakes, and endlessly jockeying for positions in a kingdom they couldn't dream of.

Yet Jesus was kind to them, despite their immaturity. In fact, regardless of their hitches and glitches, Jesus encouraged His followers to take part in the discipleship of others.

Jesus' way believed in people, in unity, in community. Jesus believed in the power of uniting people in spite, or perhaps *because,* of their differences. Both Philip Yancey and Dallas Willard have gone to great lengths to explore the diversity of Jesus' friendships and the way He related to people of different varieties. In their books—which I would recommend to any student of Jesus—they uncover the genius of Jesus in weaving together a tapestry of such diversity. The band of brothers who followed Jesus consisted of people with—get this—*different religious beliefs.* Different sects, groups that hated and feared each other. Jesus believed in the power people could wield when they converged on a common goal, a common relationship.

The importance of relationship became evident immediately after Jesus' execution. The disciples holed themselves up, not to plan a new game strategy or formulate a way to continue the kingdom without a king, but to mourn, fear, and grieve their confusion and loss. Jesus was their common thread. He was the one they all agreed on, with the notable exception of Judas (now dead), and the possible exception of Thomas, who was so shaken that Jesus later had to prove Himself to Thomas to lift his shattered hope from the ashes.

Jesus' way believed in the power of the heart over the power of the brain. Jesus believed that His followers could converge with passion, that they could come together by what was in their hearts, which would lead to changed minds.

Jesus still believes this, if it is indeed true that He never changes. Jesus cared about reaching hearts, wounded, broken, crazy, stubborn, radical hearts. Different heartbeats, different pains.

Jesus believed that faith did not necessarily arise from logical deduction, but from need, from pain, from hopelessness.

Jesus' way was the way of the heart.

Jesus was genuinely spiritual. These days, the word *spiritual* implies a maharajah, an ascetic, a monk, a Tibetan priest shrouded in orange. And yet, if we could see into the strata of spiritual mysticism, we would find Jesus sitting at the very top, undisputed master of the spiritual world.

But unlike the mystics of the other religions, Jesus' spirituality was inherent. He was it. He was the Way. Is the Way. Within His person He carried the kingdom of heaven. Paradise. Jesus believed in Himself, which drove His urgent call for others to believe in Him also. Jesus did not offer or endorse any other way, any other moral code except His own. Jesus was exclusively the Way.

Jesus' way assumes persecution. He foretold it in His teachings. Jesus' way was not a path of minimal resistance, and it was not non-confrontational. Jesus deliberately set Himself up to receive pain. He did not shy away from it, and He did not set His disciples on a fast track for pain-free success.

Jesus' way embraced death as a way of life. Not with the crudity of death worship or the flair of gothic tragedy, but as a real and important concept of the soul. This ideation of death embodies humility, true power, and of course, the bigger picture of the kingdom of heaven. This sort of martyrdom means existence in Jesus long before actual death. It is a way of living while somehow dead, somehow lost to this world.

Jesus' way is a way of great personal cost and even greater personal pleasure. It is an economy of joy and pain existing in a life lived according to the values and priorities of Jesus. Self is no longer the most important commodity. Living in the wisdom and compassion of the true Way, the life of the Nazarene, is in itself a death of sorts. It is a daily ritual of surrender to the here and now of self-interest. In order to live like this, we must model ourselves after the Christ, pursuing relationships, compassion, and even reckless self-endangerment as a sacrifice to this person, this Way. Jesus' way embraces this cost as a means of living in the pleasure of the kingdom of heaven. It is what pastor and writer/translator Eugene Peterson refers to as the "pilgrimage" of obedience to Jesus.[1] It is a journey, it is a trail, it is a way.

It is the only Way.

12

Gays, Liberals, and Muslims

I titled this chapter just to raise some tempers and a few eyebrows. Really, I did. I was having lunch with my friend Richard the other day, and as we ate, I watched his body language, the way he interacted with the people around him. Richard, as you know by now, is my friend in Colorado Springs who spends himself with earnest compassion to love, protect, and accept the people around him, many of whom are gay, most of whom are liberal.

While I watched him, I couldn't help but think that this guy has more integrity than I do. I realized there wasn't a dishonest gesture in his library. He didn't pretend to be anything other than himself. Also I realized that he had more empathy for the people around him than anyone I had seen for a long time. He accepted people, didn't judge them, and offered encouragement to everyone. He was going through a rough patch in his business and personal life, having just lost two dear friends and employees in a fatal car accident. All the while, he glowed with an earnest manner, reaching out, making friends, and loving people the way they were.

So how did I meet Richard?

Our family came back to the States from Beirut, Lebanon, where we had been living for eight years. Our stateside home had been Colorado Springs, where our small Vineyard church had sent us back in 1992. The pastor had asked me if I'd be the interim pastor until they could find a new one, as he was moving on to other things. I said yes, so we came "home" for a year.

During that time I began studying and preparing my weekly sermons at Poor Richard's, the little coffee shop/restaurant/used bookstore downtown. I had heard it was the toughest place in town. Where all the gays, Wiccans, and generally odd people hung out. So I thought, *Perfect, sounds like a place Jesus would be, so I'll go study there.*

One day I struck up a conversation with Ed, the bookstore manager. I think I was buying a couple of old Philip Yancey books (Christian-type books were always really cheap there). As Ed looked at my books and then looked at me (we had not talked before), I asked, "So … what do you think about Christians?"

It was hilarious. I'll never forget the look on his face as he tried to be nice to his customer in front of him. "Uh. Yeah. Good. No problem," he muttered, looking a bit sheepish.

I pressed him. "Come on, tell me the truth."

"Well, there was that one time that they threw a brick through our window. And when they talk bad about us on the radio. And when they preach against us outside. And ..."

It was like the dike broke when he knew I really wanted to hear. When he paused, I said, "Where do you think Jesus would be if He were here in Colorado Springs right now?"

"Focus on the Family?" he replied with a questioning tone, obviously unsure he was qualified to answer such a question.

I slapped the countertop he was standing behind and made a *ding* sound and said, "Nope. Wrong answer. You know where Jesus would be, Ed? Right here at Poor Richard's. And I'm trying to follow Him, so I try to come where He'd be."

I went on to ask if he'd ever noticed me reading the Bible in the corner. Ed said he had and was surprised, but didn't want to ask about it. I told him I prepared my talks there every week for the church I preached in on Sundays. He was *so* confused.

Then I asked him my favorite question. I said, "Ed, if Jesus came into this room right now—I mean, physically was here—who do you think He'd prefer to go hang out with, me or you?"

Like everyone else, he got the answer wrong. He said it would be me. I hit the counter again and made the negative bell sound and said, "Ed, you're not doing well. You're zero for two. Jesus would *for sure* go home with you. You need to read the book, bro."

"What book?"

"The Bible. The book about Jesus. It's all in there. He was always making religious people angry—the ones who thought they owned Him and all truth. Because He kept hanging out with people they thought were inappropriate. The sinners. Lepers. Prostitutes. Samaritans. Ed, He would choose you."

I felt so moved as I saw his response to this shocking assertion that I walked around the counter and put my hand on Ed's shoulder. I said, "Ed, Jesus is for you. He is not against you. He actually likes you. It's my type, the religious ones, who need to be careful lest we find ourselves on the very opposite side of Jesus."

He nearly began to cry. He then asked me if I was a Christian because he'd never heard a Christian say anything like this before. I explained that "being Christian" wasn't the point, but that I was actually trying to follow Jesus. He asked me if I knew Richard, the owner of the place and a city councilman. I hadn't even heard of him. We then went upstairs to Richard's office to meet him, but he was out. Ed explained our whole exchange to the secretary and the bookkeeper. They were both shocked and said, "Richard will want to hear this for sure."

The next morning at 7:30 a.m., I received a phone call at home from Richard Skorman. We had lunch that day. And a friendship began. I love the guy to death. He and his wife have become dear friends. Ten years after that first lunch, I interviewed him, and here is our conversation.

(Beginning interview)

How do you describe yourself in a sentence?

Small business owner. Former city councilman. Was the vice-mayor of Colorado Springs. Gay rights activist. Was the outspoken voice against Colorado's Amendment Two in the early '90s. An environmentalist activist. Socially liberal, but fiscally fairly conservative.

Have served on the board of the National Gay and Lesbian Foundation run by Tim Gill. Was their "token straight person." Happily married to Patricia. No kids.

Are you a Christian?

No. Culturally Jewish. From ages five to thirteen went to Hebrew school three to five days a week. Attended all the weekend services at the synagogue. Had my Bar Mitzvah at thirteen. But totally rejected Judaism and religion in general as a superstitious, silly idea. And I saw a lot of reverse discrimination—from my Jewish people toward others. We were always better than them (the Goyim/Gentiles). I always expected more from my Jewish community toward others and was disappointed by what I saw.

Give me a story or two of a negative interaction or experience you've had with Christians or Christianity.

I showed *The Last Temptation of Christ* at our private theater in Colorado Springs and got evicted and had several bomb threats. Then a bunch of death threats for showing it.

Then, because of my active support for gay rights in the Amendment Two debate, I had so many phone calls at home threatening to hurt or kill me and/or my wife.

I had a brick thrown through the window of my downtown restaurant. Written on the brick was, "It's Adam and Eve not Adam and Steve!"

A group was formed called "Citizens Against Richard Skorman." People would protest outside our shop yelling at us, while carrying a cross.

When Christians have seen me on the streets, they have told me God was angry with me and that I was going to hell.

But ... I can still say that most of my personal interactions with Christians have been positive. People have always felt comfortable talking to me about these issues from both sides.

In a sentence or two, describe our friendship.

I tell others that you are my open-minded evangelical friend. Strong values but is willing to listen. Interesting. And you've probably been the Christian in my life that has been most gracious to me.

In fact, even though I've lived in Colorado Springs most of my adult life, you were the first person to ever invite me into an evangelical church. In fact, you had me share a few words there. (We both laugh at this memory, as everyone was slightly freaked out that Richard Skorman was speaking from the front of the church.) It was an awesome experience.

In fact, I think our friendship affected me so much that when I was asked to give the main speech at the Fallen Firefighters Memorial after 9/11, I talked about the ways of Jesus and that if He lived here today He might be a firefighter. And I took a lot of flack from both sides for saying that. Some Christians said, "How dare that Skorman talk about Jesus." And some of my friends couldn't believe I brought up Jesus!

When you think of the person of Jesus, what first comes to mind?

The intrinsic value of all. Total forgiveness. Love. Kindness. Giving. One hundred percent positive!

It's the *religion* of Christianity that I don't like—not Jesus.

Can you think of anything in the way that I have approached you or spent time with you that makes you think I'm trying to evangelize or proselytize you into Christianity?

You've always been direct. I know where you stand. You ask a lot of really good questions, like "What if this or that were true ...?"

But *no.* I have never felt "evangelized" by you in the negative senses of that word. That's what I love about you and others I've met like you—I'm attracted to people who live the values they speak of and am repelled by those who don't.

So you haven't felt evangelized, but have we spent time talking about Jesus?

Yes, all the time. And it's always interesting. I know you respect me and I respect you. You have helped me understand things about Jesus that I would not have otherwise. And also have helped clarify the differences between Jesus and the negative things I've seen in Christianity.

(End interview)

One day Richard stunned me with a surprise phone call. Here's how the conversation went down.

"Carl—it's Richard. You have a minute?"

"Yep, go ahead." I poured myself a cup of coffee and settled down in the chair by the front window.

"Patricia and I are going to have some of our friends over to observe and celebrate the Passover, and we'd like to invite you and Chris to join us."

Okay, my turn to be confused. I hadn't thought of Richard and Patricia as religious in any way, but I was instantly intrigued. "Of course," I said, "we'd be honored. When and where?"

He gave me the details, and I hung up the phone. I couldn't wait to tell Chris—she'd love it.

The meal was kosher, and it was superb—Richard is an excellent chef. The company was as diverse as it could get. It seemed Chris and I were the only guests who weren't tattooed or pierced or gay. At some point in the meal we passed around a tray with crackers, and each person took a moment to stand and say something. Without exception, every single guest made some statement or another about being grateful for freedom. I could only assume most of them were talking about being free to express their beliefs or being gay. A few of them even said so. Finally, it was my turn.

Well, what does Carl do when somebody gives him the floor? He talks about Jesus, even if it is a Passover celebration, even if none of the people next to him want to hear it.

Okay, so it was a little unkosher, but I talked about my gratitude that Jesus was in my life and how Chris and I had come to believe that following Jesus was the ultimate freedom.

There was a pause as I sat down. Chris stood and shared next. I sat there with my jaw hanging down to my belt buckle—she was stunning, talking about how she discovered that Jesus is the most important friend we have, and how much she loved Him.

After supper, a young woman approached us. She started crying as soon as she opened her mouth to speak. "Listen." She took hold of my arm and looked up at me. "I used to be one of them, you know."

"One of who?" I asked.

"You people. I used to be born again. A Christian."

"Really?" I asked. "I wouldn't have guessed, but uh, tell me what happened."

She started to shake, sobbing louder. "I'm a lesbian," she said. "I fought it every step of the way too. Finally, I couldn't take it anymore. I was drowning in guilt and shame, and I was so afraid that if I told anybody about my struggle, they wouldn't understand, they wouldn't want to ever see me again."

"And?" Chris asked. I looked at her, and we both knew what was coming.

"I finally told my pastor, I asked him if there was anything he could do to help me, if there was some counselor or something. I was so desperate. I thought there was something wrong with me, and I thought it was going to kill me." She stopped crying and looked at us. Her face was pinched and sorrowful. "He told me to get out, to not come back. He said there was no place for me in the kingdom of God. He said that God hates people like me."

"I'm so sorry," was all I could say.

"Do you believe that?" Chris asked.

"I ... I don't know," she answered.

"What about Jesus?" I asked, "What do you feel about Jesus?"

"I've always tried to love Jesus, and I've always wanted Him," she said, simply.

"Well, it sounds to me like you have the main thing right," I said, "and maybe your struggle with your lifestyle is secondary."

"You think so?" she asked.

"Yes, I do."

"What's your position on gays?" she asked.

I didn't even have to think about that one. "The same as Jesus': to love them."

"Do you think there's something wrong with being gay?"

I paused for a moment—I had to think. "I have a tendency to lust," I said. "Is there something wrong with that?"

"Well of course," she said, "it's a sin."

"Does that mean that it's okay to lust?"

"No," she said, "but it doesn't mean that Jesus doesn't want to save you."

"Exactly," I said. "My faults don't keep Jesus from me, but they can keep me from Him."

"What are you saying?" she asked.

"That I don't have to change for Jesus to love me. But I do have to change if I am going to love Him back."

"You mean that your sin is no different than my sin?" she asked.

"There is no difference—sin is sin. It keeps all of us from Jesus to the point where we prefer our way to His way."

Around the same time, I accepted an invitation to guest lecture a series of classes a local college was presenting on evangelism. A church hosted the Monday night sessions, and I was pleased to find an eager, attentive adult class that was mostly full.

Halfway through the series, I could see that the group was "getting it," which only means, unfortunately, that it made sense to them. So, being the upstart that I am, I came up with a plan to introduce my friend Richard to the group, as a coteacher.

"Look," I said to him one night, "the very fact that you are seen by these kind of people as 'the enemy' is going to be our asset in this class. They are going to realize that although they want to obey Jesus and His teachings, their actions belie their beliefs."

"Okay," he said, "we're going to sneak a point in on them."

"Sort of. See, the thing that I'm trying to do here is point out that the whole sociopolitical 'Christian legislation machine' has taught people to stop looking at people as people, but instead to look at the agenda, and then to pick sides, and then to start targeting."

"And I am that target?" he asked.

"Well, you represent the gay-rights community," I said. "There are a lot of people in this town who have put you right at the top of their bad-guy list. Up on the hill, there are groups that exist just to counter all of the things you have invested yourself into."

He grinned. "And you want me to be the wolf in a classroom full of sheep?"

"Yeah," I said, "but you have to promise not to eat anyone."

I brought him to the next class, and introduced him right from the start. "Listen up, everybody, I'm going to divide up the class time and allow a dear friend of mine to speak to you. Some of you will recognize him, but for the benefit of the rest of you, I'll introduce him."

There was a slight hush when Richard stood up and came to the front.

"This is my friend Richard," I began. "He is the vice-mayor of Colorado Springs, a prominent businessman, and owner of Poor Richard's, downtown."

A slight buzz came from the class. I could see heads turning, people whispering.

"Richard is not what you might call a Christian," I said, "but, nevertheless, he is one of the most Christlike people I have ever met. He is sincere, he has integrity, and most of all, he has a deep sense of compassion for people, particularly the gay and lesbian community of Colorado Springs. Because of this, he has become something of a target to the conservative-evangelical community. Some people have even gone so far as to throw bricks through his shop windows with nasty notes attached."

A sense of anticipation and something else—excitement perhaps?—swept over the class.

"I'd like Richard to take the first half of the lecture tonight, and I want you to be respectful and attentive. Okay?"

I sat down, and there was a hush when I did. The entire class seemed to be holding its collective breath.

"Thank you, Carl," Richard said from the podium.

"Sir?" A hand rose near the middle of the class.

"Yes?" Richard responded.

I held my breath, ready for anything to happen.

A man stood up, wiped his face with his hands, and began. "I wanted to apologize to you," he said. His voice shook.

"That's really not necessary," Richard said.

"Yes it is," said the man, "it's necessary for me. I have judged you, in the past. I thought you were a bad guy, I took part in the slander and the mudslinging."

"Look, that's okay," Richard tried to say.

"No sir. It's not okay. Jesus taught us to love our enemies, and He taught us not to judge. Until I started taking this class, I spent my entire life fighting against people and policies. I fought against the homosexual movement, and I said and did things that were not right. I have disobeyed Jesus by judging you, and I wanted to say …"

The room was dead silent. You could almost hear people blinking.

"… that I'm sorry. Will you forgive me?" The man's voice cracked.

"Well, uh …" Richard's face colored, and he fingered his collar. I could see his throat working, trying to say something, but he was quiet for a minute.

Finally he spoke, and I could hear the strain in his voice from where I sat. "I forgive you," he said.

Later, as I drove home, I could feel exhilaration pumping through me. Only Jesus could make an exchange like that happen, and He had.

After that incident, I decided to make Richard's café/bookstore my permanent office. I took my laptop and my papers and set up shop near the back of the café, where I could work on this book surrounded by pierced, tattooed gay people. I love it down there.

One day I told Richard, "I really like being here at your shop. I'd like to keep coming down here to work on my projects—if that's okay with you."

"Of course," he said.

He came back by my table an hour or so later. "Here you go," he said, and fished a ring of keys out of his pocket. He set them on the table. "My shop is your shop. These are the keys to all the doors, and you can come in here any time, day or night, and do whatever you want. There's a copier and a fax machine in my office, so you can even move in there if you want to."

I was stunned. I'd just asked him if I could hang out, and he'd given me his shop. Talk about generosity, and all this from a man who is supposedly a "bad guy."

Then it hit me. What if we explored the personality of Jesus through His friendships? The people He surrounded Himself with? I read a book recently, *Jesus Before Christianity,* by Albert Nolan. He points out how Jesus differed from other figures of His time by mixing socially with all kinds of people.

"John the Baptist preached to sinners," he writes, "Hanina ben Dosa exorcised evil spirits from them. But Jesus identified with them.

He went out of his way to mix socially with beggars, tax collectors and prostitutes."[1]

Nolan goes on to describe how dining with company was the ultimate in social intimacy. It was impolite in the society of the time, and perhaps even to this day, to dine with lower classes, or to entertain someone whose lifestyle was disapproved of. Jesus constantly violated this obvious social taboo. Nolan writes,

> The scandal Jesus caused in that society by mixing socially with sinners can hardly be imagined by most people in the modern world today. It meant that he accepted them and approved of them and that he actually wanted to be "a friend of tax collectors and sinners."[2]

Can you imagine what that would look like today? Instead of promoting the talking-head formatted debates on the television and radio, what if we started inviting the gays, lesbians, liberals, and prostitutes into our houses for dinner?

The Western church is attempting to legislate morality in order to maintain a society that is pure, safe, and peaceful. Which, in and of itself, is not a bad desire.

But when injured, we change. Under fire from a hostile and misunderstanding world, we grow defensive, begin challenging and targeting different opposition groups, demolishing the characters and teachings of individuals through media outlets, pamphlets, and even sermons.

It becomes very difficult to "love the sinner, hate the sin" when we hole up in a defensive posture.

I think it's a huge mistake to turn morality into a politically, legally enforced code, because doing so creates more division and defensive posturing.

Have you ever noticed how quickly a fight or debate turns against you when you become defensive? After nineteen years of marriage, I am an expert on this situation. Many times I have come home for the evening, with chips on both shoulders, already prepped for a fight for one reason or another. If you're married, or in a serious relationship with a friend or parent, you probably know all about this.

Tension mounts, and soon an argument begins about something like the kids, finances, or how much time you spend away.

"What's wrong?" my wife asked me one day.

I slumped against the wall by the door, and waited a minute before answering her. "Nothing," I said.

"Nothing, huh?" She was drying her hands with a dish towel, looking at me suspiciously.

"Yep," I said shortly. I kicked off my shoes, went to the bathroom, and rinsed my face. Oh, what a day. I dried off, went out to the living room, and sat down in the corner of the couch.

"We the jury," Chris said as she came in and sat down on the couch opposite me, "find you guilty of fibbing. Something's wrong—out with it."

I don't like being pressed, even if I am guilty of fibbing.

"Nothing's wrong," I barked at her, "so quit bugging me, okay? Is that all right with you, huh?"

I went to the bedroom and fell backward on the bed. I stared at the ceiling.

Busted. Pure and simple.

Chris stood in the doorway with a small smile on her face. "Care to make a statement before I take you down to the station for questioning?"

I had to laugh. It was a small argument, less than five minutes in duration, yet it proved an irrefutable point. A lesson I constantly seem to be learning. As soon as you get defensive, you prove your own guilt.

And so it is with Christendom. When you fill your mind with all of the explanations, you are prepping for a fight whether you want one or not. Because, believe it or not, there are millions of people who totally disagree with you. They may even think you're an idiot, wasting your life on something you can't see, hear, feel, touch, or taste. And as you go cruising down the interstate highway of life, you're going to collide with these people: New Age practitioners, atheists, liberal Democrats, humanists, Buddhists, Muslims, etc.

Your first inclination will be to defend Christianity, which, if you have read thus far in the book, you will know is the wrong thing to do. Once you attempt to defend Christian history, you will quickly find yourself in a very difficult place. If you do choose to defend it, you will be forced to take ownership of actions that you didn't sanction and hopefully wouldn't have performed. It's simply better not to argue the point.

Not long ago I was in Denver, meeting with some old friends. One of them approached me and said, "Hey, Carl, there's a missionary couple I want you to meet."

I agreed and set up a meeting over coffee with this couple. I won't mention their names, but it was a husband-and-wife team. He was Egyptian. She was American.

"Mr. Medearis?" they said as they approached.

"That's me," I said.

"We've heard a lot about you," he said.

"Oh?"

"Yes … it seems like you're quite the fixture of conversation over there."

"Over there?"

"Yeah, um, you know … the Middle East."

I took a sip of my coffee. "So what have you heard about me, from whom?"

"Almost everybody," they said. "We have friends, acquaintances, even strangers approach us and tell us about you."

"I'm not sure that's a good thing," I said.

After some time, the conversation became serious. "Listen, Mr. Medearis, what is it that you do? How are you so effective?"

"My name's Carl—enough with the 'mister Medearis' stuff."

"Okay … Carl, what do you do? What's your method?"

"It's simple, actually," I said, and took another sip of my coffee. "I talk to people about Jesus, and not Christianity."

They both leaned back in their chairs, and a look like *oooh, man* came over their faces. "Got it," they said after a minute or two. And I could tell it had really sunk in. When you tell people this for long enough, you realize that some people get it and some people don't— they get cranky instead.

One of my favorite things to do is to invite Jesus into dinner conversations. Once a friend of mine, a doctor in Beirut, decided to host an expensive dinner at an upscale restaurant in the city. He invited Chris and me, and of course we attended. I found out afterward that the meal cost him well in excess of three thousand dollars.

During the meal, we attracted the attention of a member of Parliament who was also dining at the restaurant. After some time, he and his entire entourage came over and joined us. After they sat down there were about thirty people packed around the table. Everybody was having a great time. My doctor friend rose to his feet and said that we ought to go around the table, one at a time, each with a minute to say something.

Great. As it happened, I was the third person in line. So I got to my feet, toasted the doctor, and thanked him for the meal. I said that I was extremely grateful for the chance to live in their community, that they had taught me so much about Jesus, and that Jesus had become the most important thing to me in the whole world.

What happened next rated a flat-out ten on my funny meter.

For some reason, without exception, every person after me felt obligated to say something about Jesus. Chris and I were the only people at the table who weren't Muslim, and here, in this dining room late at night in Beirut, thirty Muslims were standing and saying openly gratuitous stuff about Jesus. I don't know if it was peer pressure or not, but it was the highlight of my week. I was in stitches all the way home. Chris thought it was funny too. "Have you ever seen anything like that?" she laughed.

"No, I haven't," I said, "but if Jesus keeps that up, we're going to need a new job in no time."

"Yeah, right," she said.

What's really intriguing to me is how simple it is to share Jesus with other people as opposed to trying to make "Christians" out of them. I remember when I was younger and just starting out, I used to ask people, "Do you believe in God?" I would spell out the master plan of salvation and do these ridiculous illustrations to convince people that it was logical to believe in God.

"See, God is like an egg," I would tell them. "There's one egg, but there are three components, and that's like God because ..."

I'm certain that every time I did that, one angel would nudge another angel as they looked down from above and say, "Hey, everybody, check this out. Medearis is doing that egg thing again."

Oh yeah—I'm telling you, I used to try to explain God's existence. With an egg, no less.

Now I sit in upper-crust restaurants and try not to laugh my head off as my Muslim friends scramble to think of the nicest things they can say about Jesus.

Yes—I'm being funny (or trying to be), but I'm making a point. Jesus is portable. No—belay that. It's not as if we're carrying Him somewhere. More the other way around. All I do is point at Him.

About a year ago, a friend and I went to Pearl Street Mall in Boulder, Colorado, with a camera crew. We decided to take a survey, and asked fifty people one question. I had the microphone and people would walk by and I'd say, "Hi, we're taking an independent survey and wondered if you had a second. It's on religion in America and we'd like to know your thoughts on Christianity."

We tried to ask in a casual way. Out of fifty people, how many would you guess were negative about Christianity? Fifty. That surprised me. I thought we might find a few that were part of the club. But the people we asked were really angry. We had to bleep out several words in the documentary. They were all negative about what Christianity represented. Then we asked fifty people what they thought about the person of Jesus of Nazareth.

Out of fifty, how many people do you think answered positively? Fifty. All fifty were positive. That amazed me. This survey confirmed that people have an issue with Christianity. But isn't it a good principle of reconciliation and mutual understanding to start where people are?

What if the message of reconciliation that all of us can agree on is actually a person—not a text, theology, doctrine, church, or religion? What if Christianity doesn't own Jesus? What if Jesus is bigger than our religion? That's disconcerting if we're used to being in a comfortable box. What if Jesus acts godlike and goes wherever He wants and takes people out of the box? What if He gives grace to sinners? What if He uses people like me to talk to people in the Hezbollah and the Hamas about Jesus?

I find that if I come in and introduce myself as Carl the Christian, the conversation is pretty much over. You can't build a real relationship or real bridge. So I come in and simply say I'm a guy named Carl and I would like to be friends, and I've been trying to follow a person, Jesus. I don't even say I'm a follower of Jesus, because that seems too presumptuous, so I say I'm trying to follow Jesus.

I actually said this to a leader in Baghdad: "We think Jesus is here because two thousand years ago, Jesus was always in the place where the religious leaders thought He shouldn't be." Isn't that true? He was always with the "wrong" people at the "wrong" time. As Christians, we're tempted to think Jesus is ours and we have Him in a box. Then we're frustrated when people allow Him out of the box.

My prayer, encouragement, and challenge for you today is to let Jesus go. Let Him out of the box you have Him in. He's bigger than our religion. This is not a message of theological universalism. This is a very practical point. I don't think that all ways are equal or all roads lead home. I believe each person finds the road through the Way Himself, Jesus.

We often blame Jesus when our evangelistic efforts fail. I hear my friends say, "Well I was out there on the streets preaching and they didn't like it, but that's what the Bible says. It says they won't like it and they didn't like it so …" I don't think it's Jesus they aren't liking. It might be you. We need to step out of the way because Jesus is interested in letting everyone in.

I'll close with this thought. My friend Sameer calls himself a Muslim who follows Jesus. It's confusing—you have to get to know him to understand. About five years ago I was talking with him in his house. He said, "Carl, I figured it out. Here's the answer for the Middle East. People come up to this house, and on the house it says 'Christianity: Do not enter.'"

I said, "That's not what the house says."

"Oh yes," he replied, "in the Middle East the house called Christianity has a subtitle and it says 'Do not enter,' 'Keep out, we are against you.'" He said, "We have to take those words off the house because it's actually not the house of Christianity. It's the house of Jesus. So here's my plan. People get close to the house and they're reading Christianity. They're ready to turn away, but we have to grab them and take them and open up the door and say, 'Look! It's Jesus.' And Jesus will invite them in because Jesus loves people. He's not the guy in the way. He is the way."

Jesus!

Appendix

The Exclusivity Question

One of the first challenges you'll encounter as you begin to share your wonderful friendship with Jesus is something like, "Are you trying to tell me that Jesus is the only way? That the pygmies in Africa are going to hell because they don't know Jesus? And what about my Buddhist friend who is clearly much nicer than you—and who never tells me that I'm going to hell or that I have it wrong? Huh?"

First of all, you would say, "I don't think I told you that you were going anywhere, let alone hell. And I also don't think I mentioned anything about Jesus being the only way, or anything about Pygmies or Buddhists. But other than that …"

But you will definitely have people assault you simply because you're speaking of Jesus—even if you're doing it in the nicest, friend-liest way known to mankind. They will hear the word *Jesus* come from your mouth. And they will assume a bunch of things based on conversations they've had in the past. Fair or not, this is what will happen some of the times you speak of Jesus to a friend, coworker, family member, or neighbor.

This will be tricky, but without getting into the theology of exclusivism (Jesus being the only way to God and salvation), I will attempt to give you some tools for such a conversation.

As always, you have choices. A popular choice, which I grew up thinking was the only correct choice, is to simply say, "Yep, sorry, He's the only way." Fair enough. Actually that's still my theology on the matter. The details of what it means that "Jesus is the only way" are not for this book—although if you're an alert reader you will find hints throughout as to what I believe.

Two problems with the "Yep, He's the only way" approach: One is that Jesus Himself typically didn't use that tactic. The other is that it's a door-closer, which is possibly why Jesus used it so seldomly.

Remember that just because something is ultimately true doesn't mean you need to say it up front in a conversation. It might be true that I have a paunch—a little overweight, let's say. But for you to introduce yourself to me and then say, "By the way, Carl, you're a bit chubby," just wouldn't be helpful—although maybe true (and I'm not saying).

Or you can go to the other extreme and say to the person something like, "Yeah, you're right, and who really knows anyway. Maybe all roads do lead to Rome/God." Now if that's what you believe, go ahead and say it. Far be it from me to encourage you to lie. Have integrity. I'd also challenge you to read the Book again to see if you're on the right track with that argument.

Or some might think like I do—that Jesus is the way—but you just don't want to say it to the person challenging you. I'd call that being a chicken. You can strategically delay the answer, which I have often done, but you can't ultimately ignore it or pretend this issue doesn't exist. For many people, how we answer the question of exclusivity determines whether they will keep listening to what we have to say.

As you may have guessed, I have another way to deal with this issue/question of whether or not Jesus is the only way (to salvation or heaven or whatever the person means).

First of all, it's always important that we're answering the real question. Jesus was brilliant at this. People are generally asking if we want them to sign up for the Christian religion and if we think our religion is the only good one. If they're asking that, but the question comes out as "Is Jesus the only way?"—to which we answer yes—then we've said yes to the real question of "Do I need to join your religion called Christianity, thus condemning all others to hell?"

This is where listening comes in handy. If you can hear what people are truly concerned about before you answer, it will save you (and them) lots of confusing conversation.

If you've agreed with my thesis that it's not about joining a religion but following a person, then you can answer the real question this way:

"I appreciate the question. It's a real one. I've asked it a lot myself and I know many others around the world struggle with wondering whether or not there is 'only one way.' And I'm pretty sure people— even top theologians from all the world's greatest religions—have been struggling with this question for centuries. So I hesitate to

give you the Final Answer with any great certainty, as if it's for the
$64,000 question on *Who Wants to Be a Millionaire?*

"So let me clarify—would you say that your question has to
do with my theology? What I believe about God? Faith? The Bible?
Jesus? All of which I'm happy to talk about. Could be a fun conversation over several beers. Or is your question more of a thought about
all the other Christians you've met in your life who seemed to know
the Final Answer and liked telling you what that was—and what you
should do about it?"

I really do want to clarify. This is not a stalling tactic because
the question scares me. Not at all. I need to hear, really hear what
they're asking. Most of the time they don't really know exactly what
they're asking or why. And that's okay. But let's imagine it's a defen-
sively postured question based on past hurts, with a little bit of "I
wonder what Carl thinks about this" mixed in. Then this would be
my answer:

"Here's the thing. Jesus is good. He is good news. He doesn't just
know some good news. He is the good news. Have you ever heard
the term *the gospel?* Probably. It gets used as something to preach at
sinners, but how it was used in the Bible and by Jesus Himself was
to proclaim this new way of living and loving and being loved—the
good news of Jesus. That's what He does for us. Gives us life. Heals
and restores us. Provides answers, truth, a way to live forever. All
good things.

"You've also probably heard the word *repent* and wondered why
those gospel preachers are demanding that you repent. Actually the
word *repent* just means to turn around and start going in the right
direction. When you're lost on the road (not that I would ever be

lost, but maybe you have been) then you'd be 'repenting' when you turn around and go the right way. Jesus says we should do that and follow Him because it's good for us. It's the right thing to do—not to sign up for a certain religious identity, but to have life. Real and full life. Good news indeed.

"So is He the only way to that kind of good news for everyone? I think so, but I'm happy to be wrong about that. If you find pygmies and Buddhists and Hindus and Muslims and people who call themselves Christians who have somehow found that fulfillment outside of Jesus—great. I'm not here to say who's in and who's out. I'm not God. But as far as I can tell, Jesus is the best news around and everyone that I've ever told about Him seems to like Him. Some even choose to follow Him and commit themselves to His way. But it's totally your choice. No pressure from me!

"And please don't ever think that God is up in heaven on His big white throne, with His long gray beard and big iron scepter in His hand just waiting to smack someone who goes awry. That's such a faulty picture of God. Jesus told us the real picture in Luke chapter fifteen. It's a picture of God running to the sinner who has turned to come crawling back home—but God can't wait for him, so He runs to the kid and hugs him. Kisses him. Rewards him and welcomes him home. That's the real God. And that's what we and everyone else get when we say yes to Jesus. Good news, man. I'm telling you, it's good news!"

Notes

Chapter 1: What's Missing in This Gospel?

1. Donald Miller, *Searching for God Knows What* (Nashville: Thomas Nelson, 2004), 158.
2. Ibid.
3. Ibid., 159.
4. Ibid.
5. Ibid.

Chapter 3: Owning Christianity

1. E. Stanley Jones, *The Christ of the Indian Road* (Nashville: Abingdon, 1925), 12.
2. Ibid.
3. Ibid.

4. Donald Miller, *Blue Like Jazz* (Nashville: Thomas Nelson, 2003), 115.

Chapter 4: In or Out

1. Donald Miller, *Blue Like Jazz* (Nashville: Thomas Nelson, 2003), 115.
2. Dallas Willard, *The Divine Conspiracy* (San Francisco: HarperCollins, 1998), 37.
3. Ibid.

Chapter 5: What Would Paul Say?

1. Martin Luther, quoted in Philip Yancey, *The Jesus I Never Knew* (Grand Rapids, MI: Zondervan, 2002), 72.

Chapter 7: Our Religion Can Beat Up Your Religion!

1. Todd M. Johnson, David B. Barrett, and Peter F. Crossing, "Christianity 2011: Martyrs and the Resurgence of Religion," *International Bulletin of Missionary Research* 35, no. 1 (January 2011), 29.
2. Ibid.
3. Barna Group, "49 Million Born Again Adults Shared Their Faith in Jesus in the Past Year," July 28, 2003, http://www.barna.org/barna-update/article/5-barna-update/125-49-million-born-again-adults-shared-their-faith-in-jesus-in-the-past-year.
4. T. Johnson, "USA Religion Table," in *Encyclopedia Britannica Book of the Year 2010* (Encyclopædia Britannica: 2010), 2011.

Chapter 11: Confused about Jesus … and That's Okay!

1. Eugene Peterson, *A Long Obedience in the Same Direction* (Downers Grove, IL: InterVarsity, 2000), 166.

Chapter 12: Gays, Liberals, and Muslims

1. Albert Nolan, *Jesus Before Christianity* (Maryknoll, NY: Orbis, 2001), 45.

2. Ibid.